D0188463

She Flew Bombers

From the Factories to the Bases During World War II

A historical fiction

— Second Edition —

Jeane Slone

PRAISE FOR JEANE SLONE'S
SHE FLEW BOMBERS

She Flew Bombers is a funny, sad and heroic story about the strength of one woman, Violet Willey, and her WASP (Women Airforce Service Pilots) colleagues, a colorful assortment of other patriotic women, each one strong in her own way. Women pilots were an exotic and unappreciated item during WWII, and as such, had to fight their own battles against gender discrimination before it became a problem. The same was not true of Russian women pilots, as Violet finds out in the course of delivering a Pursuit airplane to the self-proclaimed "Night Witches," as those extraordinary women combat pilots were called, because they made their aerial raids under cover of darkness. Flying a dizzying variety of airplanes was a constant challenge of WASP pilots, as well as the terrifying problem of sabotage. Add to this the knowledge that many of the planes they flew were relatively untested as they came off the assembly line, and the reader will easily understand the origin of the term, "Flying by the seat of their pants!"

— Mary Lynn Archibald
Author of *Accidental Cowgirl: Six Cows,*
No Horse and No Clue.

She Flew Bombers is a fascinating account of one woman's love of flying and her involvement with the Women Airforce Service Pilots during World War II. Anyone interested in aviation history, women's history, or the World War II "war effort" will appreciate Jeane Slone's careful research, as well as her ability to bring this little-known aspect of U.S. history to life so vividly.

— Jean Hegland, author of
Into the Forest and *Windfalls*

Author Jeane Slone does an outstanding job in her new novel, *She Flew Bombers*. This well-written and fast-paced book chronicles the history of the Women Airforce Service Pilots (WASPs) through the personal experiences of aviatrix Violet Willey. This Civil Service Organization transported all types of military aircraft across country to bases so male American flyers could be freed up to do the job of winning the war. Violet's passion for flying is documented from her first experience as a young girl going on a flight with a California barnstormer to joining the WASPs and flying Pursuits. Little seems to be written about this heroic group of women, who through their entire existence did not achieve military status until 1977. The obstacles and biases they managed to overcome as women pilots during their service to our country are expertly put to paper by author Jeane Slone. Written with humor, emotion, and accuracy, this film-worthy story will be enjoyed by anyone interested in military and aviation history, a plain good book, or a fast read.

— Tony Lazzarini, President, Military Writers Society

She Flew Bombers
From the Factories to the Bases During World War II
Copyright 2012 by Jeane Slone
Second edition
ISBN: 978-0-9838154-0-2
Library of Congress Control Number: 2011938136

Printed in the United States of America

Walter J. Willey Book Company

Cover Design: Jelehia Ziemba/Word Art/Sebastopol, California Web Site: jz@zwordart.com

This historical novel is based entirely on fact. The characters have been fictionalized.

Photo Credits

1. Aerial photography of the Curtiss Jenny and B-25 bomber courtesy Roger Cain, aerial photographer (cover)

2. Curtiss Jenny — courtesy Roger Cain , aerial photographer (page 7)

3. Yellow Piper Cub — Public Domain (page 13)

4. Barnstormers — courtesy The Museum of Flight, Seattle, WA (page 21)

5. Bombing Pearl Harbor — by Joe Fitzgerald, age 8, 1944, from Maritime Child Development Center, Courtesy Richmond Museum of History, Richmond, CA (page 45)

6. Avenger Field — courtesy United States Air Force Museum (page 79)

7. Zoot suits, Size 44 men's surplus coveralls — courtesy National Archives (page 86)

8. Zoot suits — Public Domain (page 86)

9. Primary Trainer — Public Domain (page 89)

10. Calisthenics — courtesy National Archives (page 92)

11. Instructor and student — Public Domain (page 93)

12. Florence Emig Wheeler, Link Trainer — Public Domain (page 105)

13. Parachute pack — courtesy National Archives (page 112)

14. Parachuting — Public Domain (page 114)

15. Classroom engine: Taking an engine apart — courtesy National Archives (page 117)

Dedication

To Florence Emig Wheeler (Floss), who graduated as a WASP in 1944, and was a former flight instructor at the San Jose Airport.

I am grateful for all her support and patience in spending hours going over all the technical aspects of the book — with many cups of hot cocoa!

Acknowledgments

Florence Emig Wheeler, WASP, class of 44-W-10, Healdsburg, CA; Jean Hegland, Santa Rosa Junior College, creative writing instructor and "cheerleader"; Muriel R. Reynolds, WASP, class of 44-7, Santa Rosa, CA; Frank Schelling, owner, WWI Curtiss Jenny airplane, one of only 10 that are still currently airborne, Pleasanton, CA; Donald Basin, executive director, Richmond Museum of History, Richmond, CA; Robin Reid, 747 commercial airline pilot; William and Adele Slone, WWII Army veterans; Thomas Slone, "computer wizard"; Glenn Kerbein, technical assistant; The Healdsburg Literary Guild; George Connors, WWII pilot, Healdsburg, CA; Charley Taylor, technical advisor, former Navy pilot, member of the Pacific Coast Air Museum; Dragonfly Aviation, Santa Rosa, CA; Roger Cain, aerial photographer; Redwood Writers Club, Santa Rosa, CA; Vintage Aircraft Company, Sonoma, CA; Healdsburg Municipal Airport, Healdsburg, CA; Laurel Olson Cook, author; Cris Wanzer, *Manuscripts To Go*, editor; Sivani Lloyd, avid reader and best friend; The Sonoma Paddle Club; and my family.

Contents

Introduction

In 1942, after the war broke out, a shortage of manpower took place. Airplanes were badly needed to fly into combat. Nancy Love and Jacqueline Cochran were pioneer aviators—leaders—who employed women pilots to fly military airplanes from the factories to the bases to speed the progress of winning the war. This book pays tribute to all the daring, courageous, and spirited young women who put their lives on the line. These women, thrown into a man's world, were a contributing factor to the success of the war.

Chapter One: The Fabric and Wood Flying Machine

What was that deafening noise coming from the sky? It sounded much like Daddy's tractor. More like three of them.

The rattling, thundering racket caused Dad to run outside like an excited kid. As I tailed behind him, Mother yelled out the door for me to come help her clean the house. I skipped faster and pretended not to hear. A barnstormer flew over our farmhouse in his open-cockpit plane, and drew our attention by purposely pumping the throttle. We waved our arms high above our heads as the Curtiss Jenny slowed and glided toward the pasture. We hiked toward the magical mechanical invention.

Dad pulled out five one-dollar bills from the pocket of his well-worn coveralls for a ride in the JN-4 biplane. I felt lucky to be seven. My brothers, Tommy and Howie, were too little to go. The ear-splitting sound of the plane stopped as it landed. The pilot pushed himself up on the dark-brown leather rim of the oval cockpit. He threw one leg out, and balanced between the spider web maze of piano wires. He clutched the wood posts between the wings to get his other leg out, placed one foot in front of the other on a narrow metal strip on the bottom wing,

1

ducked the top wing, then jumped to the ground. Dad handed him the money and they shook hands.

"Harry Willey. This is my daughter, Violet. Thanks for stopping."

"Frank Billings, my pleasure." The heavily mustached pilot gave me a wink. "Ready for a ride?"

"Yesss!" I said, sounding like a snake.

The pilot handed Dad a well-used leather cap and a pair of heavy, lopsided oval glasses.

Frank grinned at me. "I don't have an extra helmet for you, young lady, but here are some goggles."

He put them over my eyes, but they fell quickly down around my neck. We all laughed.

"I guess they don't make 'em for little girls," Dad said.

I pushed the goggles back up and held them in place. "I'll make 'em work."

While Dad chatted with the barnstormer pilot, I worried that soaring up in the sky would be like riding the rickety roller coaster at the county fair. The creaking noise it made frightened me when it swung back and forth and jerked about. Once, when I got stuck at the top of it, I couldn't wait for my turn to get off.

The pilot peered at me through his goggles. "Stand over there, so your dad and I can turn the airplane around away from the farmhouse."

I moved out of the way. Dad grabbed the handholds

on one side of a wing and the pilot grabbed them on the other. My eyes opened wide watching them turn the heavy, long-winged airplane around.

"We're almost ready. Lift your daughter onto the wing. Violet, be very careful to stay on the wingwalker— that's the metal strip. It prevents your feet from tearing the fabric on the wing."

Dad held me in his long, strong farmer arms, lifted me up high onto the bottom wing, and boosted me into the back cockpit. He squeezed in behind me and I sat on his lap. Dad took the thick, white, webbed-cloth strap and fastened the metal clasp to secure us into the tiny cockpit. "Honey, stop wiggling."

"Sorry, Daddy. I'm so excited!" My smile stretched across my face.

The pilot went up to the nose of the Jenny, reached up with his muscular arms, and pulled on the wooden propeller. It took a few hard spins before the engine roared to life. He ducked between the wings, twisted around the cables to get into the front cockpit, then turned back to see how we were doing. When he saw our grins, he put his thumb up into the air. The aircraft began to creep across the uneven pasture and gained speed. A strong wind blew across the cockpit as our bumpy ride became faster and faster, the wind roaring in my ears, keeping time with my pounding heart. I squeezed Daddy's knees as the wheels left the ground and we were airborne.

I loved the sensation of my long, blond hair blowing about until I found it whipping into Daddy's face. With one hand, I wrapped my hair into a long knot, and then tucked it into the collar of my shirt. Tired of pushing the large goggles against my face, I let them slip down. A full blast of wind made my eyes tear. I stuck the goggles back on again.

I leaned back on Daddy's lap and listened to the power of the airplane. The trees in our pasture became smaller the higher we went. Our great big farmhouse turned into a magical, itty-bitty box. I closed my eyes and pretended to be a bird. Much to my delight, being in the airplane was not like the shaky roller coaster ride. The loud, humming noise of the engine made it impossible to talk, letting loose my imagination. I became a dreamy pinwheel, breezing around and around, gently soaring above the ghost-like clouds. When I opened my eyes, I saw San Jose stretched out before me—green and brown, irregular squares with tiny cows grouped about. Orchard after orchard passed under us. The small airplane's shadow followed on the side.

The ride was not long enough. Before I knew it, we came down closer to the cows near the haystacks. The noise of the Jenny made them scatter away. Oh, how I loved that "coming down from the sky" feeling. All the landmarks came into view and formed into the proper size as we glided into the field.

"Thanks Daddy, you're the best!" I said as he helped me climb out. I kissed his cheek, then scrambled over to one of the haystacks and climbed on top of it. I kicked my legs to and fro into the spiky hay that poked into my coveralls. I listened to my father talk with the pilot.

Dad said to Frank, "You said that you've had this Curtiss Jenny in your family for how many years?"

"My father flew it in World War I, but he never saw any military action. He was an aerial observer in 1918 during Brigadier General John J. Pershing's Punitive Expedition into Mexico."

"You mean, the expedition to capture that criminal?"

"Yes, Pancho Villa, who preyed on U.S. towns along the Mexican border. I don't know if they ever found him. Family rumor has it that my father smuggled a load of whiskey across the Mexican border and made eight grand."

"I'll be darned! You've got quite a famous airplane, and it's in great shape." Dad added a little whistle.

"Thanks, sir. I work on it every chance I get." The pilot shaped the ends of his mustache.

"What's the maximum speed on her?"

"It can get up to 75 miles per hour."

"Not bad."

Frank tugged on his dark-brown leather helmet. He fastened the dangling strap under his chin, then wrapped the wide, thick goggles around his face. "I must be off. I've got to find more passengers to give rides to. Gas money. Nice talking with you."

Mr. Billings took off in his Jenny. We waved and watched him accelerate into the sky. He did two rolls, one after another.

I gasped. "Going upside down looks scary, but I'd like to try it!"

Dad laughed while smoothing back a patch of his thin brown hair. "Sounds like you're catchin' the flying bug, like me."

I ran back to the farmhouse and tried to tell Mother what it was like up in the sky.

She cut me off. "Being in that dirty plane all squished in is not very ladylike. Go wash up and help me peel potatoes."

I knew then I could only share my excitement for flying with Daddy. I didn't say another word, and scrubbed the potatoes, quite content in my fantasy world of airplanes.

After I helped clean up dinner, I played with my doll, Sarah. She fit nicely in the cockpit of my model airplane. Uncle Walt had given it to me for my sixth birthday. Today, at last, I got to experience a ride in a real plane. Being up in the Jenny was scary at first, but once among the clouds, I didn't want to come down.

"Can we go again?" I asked Dad as I rolled my toy airplane about.

"You never know when a barnstormer will come by. Listen every day for their buzzing, and then come get me.

I love flying as much as you do." Dad folded up his newspaper and smiled at Mother. "Martha, let's drive out to the airport and watch the takeoffs next Sunday."

"No, I have pies to make for the church picnic." She straightened the red rickrack on the apron that covered her floral dress.

Dad winked at me, letting me know that maybe he would get his way. Being only seven, I wasn't sure which of my parents would win this argument.

Chapter Two: A Yellow Piper Cub

Flying. I lived, ate, drank, and dreamt about flying. The summer of my high school senior year I found a job in the cannery, and saved the four dollars a week I earned working there to take flying lessons at the local airport. I convinced Dad to go along with my ruse of pretending I worked all day on Saturday. That way, Mother wouldn't find out about the lessons. She would have been horrified to see me at the controls of a plane.

On the first Saturday, I anxiously looked at the clock high on the wall in the cannery. Only one more hour to go and I would get my first instructions in flying. I was the "syruper" at the factory, and it was hard on my hands. Hoisting huge, #10 cans full of sliced peaches from the syrup machine to the capping machine was slippery. The gloves the office provided were useless, and caused even more slippage. It was painstaking work. My bare hands tended to get cut up on the rims of the cans if I worked too fast.

When my flying hour arrived, I got on a bus in front of the cannery.

"Where to, miss?" the blue-capped driver asked.

"To the airport, please." My fingers twitched as I reached into my purse for the bus fare. I watched intently out the window at the new sights as we lumbered toward the airport. At last, up ahead a large wooden sign announced in black lettering: San Jose Municipal Airport. An American flag flapped above it. When the driver announced where we were, I could feel my heartbeat pounding in my chest.

I saw a small office building, but could only stand in front of it, trying to get up the courage to go inside. I talked myself toward the entrance by remembering the glorious feeling of my flight in the Jenny when I was seven.

With a deep breath, I went up the steps and pulled open the heavy office door. A man with very thick, wavy, light-brown hair, who looked younger than Dad, stood behind the counter.

"Can I help you, young lady?"

"I'm here for flying lessons," I said, looking everywhere but in his eyes.

He sized me up with an apprehensive look. "How old are you and do you have the money?"

I wound one of my blond pigtails around my finger. "I'm 17 and I've been saving up for lessons."

"Have you ever been up in an airplane?"

I stared him straight in his eyes. "I've been in a Curtiss Jenny a few times and have always wanted to learn to fly."

My last statement sparked him into saying, "Name's

Mr. Schelling. If you have the four dollars, I'm happy to give you a lesson."

He handed me paperwork to complete, explaining that after 35 hours of flying time, I would receive a license. I opened the latch of my black suede bag. With shaky fingers, I reached into my coin purse and presented the money to him. I read over the papers and carefully filled them out on the dark wooden counter.

Mr. Schelling scanned the forms. "Okay, Miss Willey. Put your things in that locker over there and follow me out to the hangar."

I glanced at an ornate sign on the wall: **May all of your winds be gentle and landings be safe.** The placard calmed my nerves.

I followed him meekly outside. Just looking out at the runway gave me a thrill. The sound of several small planes taking off brought back the exciting memory of my first flight in the Jenny. I breathed in the slight scent of oil, rousing my passion for flying even more.

We entered a semi-circular metal hangar with a banner that covered the front which read: Schelling Flying Service. Mr. Schelling began his lecture, his hands in the pockets of his brown, stained coveralls.

"This is a Piper J-3 Cub. It's 22 feet long and stands almost seven feet tall. It has a Lycoming 65-horsepower engine, and can attain a maximum speed of 85 miles per hour with a ceiling of 11,500 feet. The fuel tank holds 12 gallons, which is sufficient to fly for four hours. There have been about 3,000 of these honeys built already."

While my instructor (just the sound of the word gave me a tingle) talked to me about the Piper Cub, I compared it to the Jenny. The Curtiss Jenny was five feet longer. The Cub could go 10 miles per hour faster, which I looked forward to experiencing. I wondered how much fuel the Jenny held. Maybe I could find out the next time I met up with a barnstormer. The Jenny was a biplane, whereas the Piper Cub only had one set of wings. At least the Cub had brakes, unlike the Jenny, which only had a tail skidder to stop it. The canary yellow color of the Piper Cub struck me—how marvelous! The Jenny was basic Army olive drab. It had heavy crisscross cable wires running at all different angles—a meticulous maze of rigging between the two wings with spruce wood struts. The Cub, on the other hand, was a neater package.

I realized I was caught up in my thoughts and was not paying attention to Mr. Schelling. I straightened up my posture, which Mother always reminded me to do, and refocused on what he was saying.

"Are you ready for your first lesson?" Mr. Schelling drummed his fingers on the wing of the plane.

"Yes, Mr. Schelling."

My heart fluttered as we approached the Cub.

Mr. Schelling pulled a tiny, silver handle, opening a small, yellow, rectangular door. "Climb in the back."

I couldn't believe how easy it was to get in compared to the Jenny, though not being very tall, I did have to do a little jumping to get inside. As I sat in the back trainer seat with my strap on, I noticed the Cub had the same wooden hand-propped propeller as the Jenny did.

Mr. Schelling pulled the adorable yellow plane out of the hangar, gave the propeller several strokes, and climbed into the seat directly in front of me. Next he latched the Plexiglas window by pulling it up, fastened the door, and off we sailed. The Cub had a quiet sound, but still gave my insides quite a stir.

I tried to listen to all the new strange words, like *rudder, stick, altimeter, oil pressure gauge, and tachometer.* He shouted these words behind him. I couldn't follow everything he said. The exhilaration of flying in the Cub distracted me from hearing all the information that Mr. Schelling explained. After all, I still didn't even know how to drive an automobile. Mother probably would not have approved of that, either.

Our flight was too short. After we landed, I reluctantly followed my instructor back to the office. He hung his worn helmet on a coat hook and reached out for mine.

"Next week we'll go over the preflight checklist, as long as you have the money." Mr. Schelling cocked his head and raised one eyebrow.

"I hope to," I frowned.

"Also, Miss Willey, your height is a bit of a problem. Bring a cushion next time. You do have a lot of tenacity for a young girl. I hope I can help you get your license."

His words boosted my faith, though I didn't know

what "tenacity" meant.

"Thanks for instructing me," I said, feeling very awkward, and went to the locker to avoid further discussion.

On the bus ride home, my mind was filled with thoughts. I sure loved that plane; it moved much smoother than the Curtiss Jenny. Its spectacular, sunny-yellow color was cheerier than the boring Army color, but I'd bet the Jenny performed stunts easier. I would ask Mr. Schelling about that. I wondered if I had enough money for more lessons. College tuition would be due soon. I had to calculate my financial situation when I got home. Dad had promised to keep my flying a secret, but Mother would find out if he lent me money, and that would be the end of my dream of being a famous aviatrix.

Chapter Three: The Handsome Barnstormer

While sitting on our creaking porch swing after church several months later, I heard a heavenly buzzing sound. I ran out and flailed my arms as a barnstormer landed in the back pasture. Much to my surprise, it was someone I knew—Glenn, who had graduated from my high school a year ahead of me. I had seen him at church a few times. Dad told me that after World War I, Curtiss Jenny planes were mass produced and reasonably cheap to buy. At church, Glenn's parents appeared to be quite well dressed. Because he was an only child, his family probably had the extra money to buy him one.

Glenn yanked off a cracked, brown leather helmet, combed back his black hair, and placed his goggles on top of his head. He climbed out of the cockpit and walked off the wing. "I was surprised to see you signaling me down. Not many girls are interested in airplanes."

"I'm the kind of gal who is," I said, grinning coquettishly, noticing his muscular arms in his stylish, ribbed gray sweater. "I'd love a ride." I wanted desperately to experience stunts the barnstormers did that my lessons at the airport would never cover.

"What would your parents say about going up?"

14

"My mother doesn't even know I've been taking flying lessons, but my dad's behind me 100 percent." I worried that Dad would not approve of me being alone with a boy my age in a plane, but I kept that thought a secret.

"Really, you're taking flying lessons?" Glenn's eyes widened. "What would your mom do if she found out?"

"She thinks airplanes are dangerous. I'm the oldest and only girl in my family and my mother expects me to work around the house all day. Dad's as crazy about planes as I am, but he can't even get her to watch the takeoffs at the airport."

"Maybe we should wait to go up in the Jenny until you get permission from your parents." Glenn faced the plane, ready to get back in.

"But... this is the perfect day for me to go up with you. My mother's busy making pies for the church social. She'll never notice I'm gone."

"Doesn't she need your help?" He put his hand on the wingwalker.

"Mrs. Rosenberg's coming over to help her." I tapped my foot impatiently in the grass. "Please, Glenn, I bet you're a great pilot!"

"All right, doll face, climb in. I'll show you some new stunts I learned."

My face glowed with enthusiasm as Glenn found an old wooden tomato box in the pasture for me to use to climb up onto the wingwalker.

"Wait a minute, I've gotta get something." I ran through the field, quietly crept up the front steps of my house, and slipped inside to steal a chair cushion. Mrs. Rosenberg was chatting with Mother in the next room. After hearing her ask about me, I grabbed the cushion and hightailed it back to the pasture as fast as I could.

"Nice cushion you got there, shorty!" Glenn chuckled. "Did you see your mom?"

"She was busy with Mrs. Rosenberg in the kitchen, but Dad gave me permission to go," I lied, averting my eyes and running my fingers over the tight fabric on the Jenny's wing.

I stepped up on the tomato box and walked across the wing with my cushion. I did the "Jenny dance," hiking up into the cockpit by twisting around the wires and wood posts between the two wings. Then, I balanced on the narrow, metal wingwalker to get into the seat.

Glenn went to the front of the Jenny and pulled the propeller several strokes to start the engine. After climbing in, he grinned and yelled above the roaring engine, "Strap in, Violet. If you become afraid of my stunts and want to go back, put your hand in the air flat and wave it back and forth. Give me a high thumbs-up if you like 'em and want more. Are you ready for a few tricks?"

Beaming back at Glenn, I gave him a high thumbs-up. I found an extra helmet and goggles in the back cockpit and pulled the safety strap over my waist.

16

As we began our flight, I tried to guess where we were according to the tiny landmarks. The glorious Santa Cruz Mountains spread below us; green redwoods displayed mounds of many depths. Glenn warmed up by doing a simple S turn, but the lazy eight really impressed me. I had read a book on aerobatics, and tried to guess which tricks he was doing. The gliding of the plane gave me a warm, glowing sensation as I slouched into my seat.

All of a sudden, I felt a lurching pressure on my shoulders and stomach as we headed straight up toward the sky like a rocket in slow motion. The wind from the open cockpit pushed my body forcefully against my seat. The once beautiful scenery of the earth left my vision as gravity pressed against me. My stomach rolled. I grabbed for the front leather rim above the controls to hold myself in as we turned upside down. Sweat beaded all around my helmet. I strained to open my eyes, but fear kept them safely closed. Upon opening them, there before me I saw only blue sky and puffy clouds—no land in sight. Time stood still. I inhaled and exhaled rapidly, praying for the secure land to arrive in my vision. With sticky hands, I held on to the cockpit. At last, the earth appeared at goofy angles, but I felt completely disoriented. Finally, the pressure subsided as we straightened out. Solace came to me as we returned to the gentle cruising I adored. My pulse reverted back to normal and I released my grip.

I didn't want to reveal my anxiety about the aerobatics to Glenn. I wanted to think I had the ability to be a great woman aviator. Sucking in a deep breath, I turned around and pushed my hand under my elbow, forcing a high thumbs-up. Inwardly, I told myself to be brave. My signal gave Glenn the go ahead; he dipped the wings into a slow roll, turning the sky into land and back to sky again. Two barrel rolls in succession made me squeal with excited joy. The force on my body froze me in place as we made a complete turnaround. My stomach churned as I grabbed at the air for something to hold on to. On the second barrel roll, I knew I would stay in place. I began to relax. *Golly*, I thought over my pounding heart, *I survived that one – and even enjoyed it!* Just when I worried that we might do another frightening inverted trick, I saw that we were flying on a straight, level course. The farmhouse appeared below, and the pasture came securely toward us.

"That was fun!" I yelled above the engine as loud as I could, even though my emotions were still in an upheaval.

Glenn glanced over his shoulder and flashed a grin. He made a slow, smooth landing as the tail dragger plowed a neat furrow into the field and brought the Jenny to a stop. Two hours in the airplane with the constant noise of the engine was long enough for me, as I felt dizzy and a bit nauseated. After we twisted and turned to get out of the cockpit, Glenn put the wheel chocks on to make sure the plane wouldn't move from any sudden wind. His leather helmet strap dangled below his wide, angular chin, emphasizing his smile. He pushed his metal-rimmed goggles up on the top of his forehead, and with his hands on his hips said, "How'd you like my stunts?"

I tried walking, but swayed so much I had to sit down. Keeping my goggles on, I hid my leftover fear behind them. "What, um, were the names of the tricks we did?" I stuttered.

"What's the matter, Violet? Did I frighten you?" He leaned down and rubbed my shoulder affectionately.

"I liked most of them, but the horizontal upside-down one really shook me up."

"Darn, I forgot to tell you how to cope with gravity and the sensation of weightlessness. " His face took on a serious look.

Glenn proceeded to explain to me how to prevent motion sickness when the plane was upside down. "You need to fix your gaze on a point on the horizon, and keep staring at the ground as it disappears." To deal with the weightlessness, he told me to always look straight ahead and tighten my stomach muscles.

After taking off my goggles, my embarrassment faded. I stood up. "What are the names of all the stunts we did?"

"The one that causes the most disorientation, unless you fix your gaze right, is the loop; the one before that was a barrel roll."

"I loved that one!" I broke into an enthusiastic smile.

Glenn laughed. "So, you want to be Amelia Earhart, do ya now?"

"Actually, I want to be better than the 'Speed Queen' and more like Mabel Cody," I said, straightening out the bows on my braids. "Did you know that in her flying circus, she started from a motorboat, then climbed up a ladder into a flying Jenny?"

"I read about Mabel Cody. She's related to Buffalo Bill Cody. I'd think you'd rather be like Gladys Ingle. She was famous for shooting arrows from one wing to a target on the other, while the Jenny was flying. Why, she even shot a rifle backwards over her shoulder looking into a mirror at a target, Annie Oakley style!"

"I'd be happy just to learn to do a barrel roll." I giggled and held out a few dollars. "Here's some gas money, and thanks Glenn, it was worth the experience. I imagine my instructor won't be teaching me any aerobatics. Could you show me how to do a barrel roll someday?"

"I can't take any money, it's illegal. The daredevil days of the barnstorm era were over 13 years ago."

When I asked Glenn what he meant, he explained that the Federal Air Commerce Act of 1926 had banned dangerous aerial acrobatics. After that, everyone had to get a license to fly. Taking passengers up for joyriding was banned in 1928. I hung on every word he said as I stuffed the money back into my pocket.

Glenn continued in his know-it-all pace of talking. "There have been over 179 accidents and 90 deaths since barnstorming began. The shows I do are sensational, but I'm extremely careful in every move I make," he said, dusting some dirt off the wing of his Jenny.

"I've read a lot about flying circuses in my *Air Today* magazines. I would've loved to have been in one," I said, trying to make an impression. Glenn continued bragging, but the way he looked at me gave me the distinct feeling he was also flirting. My whole body quivered — something I had never felt before.

"I know what you mean. I've read quite a bit about barnstormers myself. I wish I could've been a pilot back then. My favorite is Clyde 'upside down' Pangborn. What a master aviator! He hung by his feet — in the air! — from the landing gear of a Jenny in the Gates Flying Circus. I love my plane and I'll do what I can within the law to keep flyin' her." He hooked his thumbs in his worn trousers.

In the 1920s, barnstormers performed wild stunts, such as this upside-down attempt to grab a hat.

"I'd love to help you in your shows," I begged, grabbing hold of his arm.

"How many hours have you logged in?" He squeezed my hand in the crook of his arm.

"Five," I said, holding my fingers up, smiling.

"Get some more hours in, then maybe I'll let you fly her," he said with a little hesitation in his voice.

I looked at the Jenny longingly and noticed a letter painted on the upper wing. "What's that?" I pointed.

Glenn grinned with a bright smile. "I painted my last name on each upper wing. Here, I'll show you."

When he lifted me up by my waist, his touch sent an electric tingle through my body. I saw "Conney" painted in big red letters on each wing.

After placing me back down on the ground, I could see by his flushed face that he felt the same way I did.

"Why'd you put your last name on the upper wings when no one will see them?" I asked.

He pushed out his chest. "People can see it when I fly upside down, like Clyde Pangborn did in 1915."

"How clever!" I held his gaze.

Glenn laughed and looked into my eyes. We shared the same passion for flying. "A girl in my show could boost sales. I always scout around for a kid to pass the can around when I fly above town; that way I'm not taking the money directly, to be legal. My dad did pay for the plane, but I still need to cover maintenance and gas money."

"I'm full of ideas and I'd love to help you."

"All right, my little aviatrix," he flirted. "Meet me next Sunday in my cow pasture. I'll draw you a map on how to get there. Come at seven in the morning, and we'll see what we can work up together."

"You can count me in!" I swung one of my braids and batted my eyelashes.

After he drew a map, Glenn removed the wheel chocks and put them into the back cockpit. He hand-propped the propeller, wing-walked into the front, pushed the throttle forward, and off he went with a wave and a grin.

As I tiptoed up the front porch steps, I hoped and prayed Mother was still in the kitchen. Then I could sneak into my bedroom without her noticing. Dad was nowhere to be seen.

Chapter Four: Solo in a Piper Cub

Placing my ear on my bedroom door, I heard my parents arguing. *I sure hope Dad defends me,* I thought as I bit one of my pigtails.

"Harry, it's just not ladylike to fly, and it's downright dangerous doing those dreadful daredevil tricks. Barnstormers have been hurt—even killed—because of their reckless activity. Violet will never find a proper husband with you allowing her to continue this flying escapade!"

"Martha, get with the times. My cousin's daughter won the eight-day race to Cleveland, while Amelia Earhart only came in third. Shirley was even in the first Women's Air Derby!"

I heard my mother sigh with dissatisfaction. "I thought Violet was going to work this morning and then before you know it, Mabel down the road rang me up and told me she was flying around town in an airplane. How will she pay for college if she misses work?"

"Dear, you know Violet is a hard worker. Let her have some fun once in a while."

Peeking out my bedroom door, I saw Mother glaring at Daddy. She threw her hands up in the air, ending the conversation with her usual Irish exclamation—"God save us!" — and went into the kitchen to do the dishes.

Dad retreated into the living room to smoke his cigar. I heard the Zenith as he tuned into the news.

"Poland has been invaded by Germany. Britain and France have declared war!"

"Martha, come quick and listen to this broadcast!" Dad said.

I eased out of my room and stood in the hallway to hear what was going on.

"France will be sending troops to Poland to come to their aid," the radio blared as Dad turned it up louder.

"I hate to say it, but it sounds like this is the beginning of World War II," Dad said. I heard him tap his wedding ring with fervor on the marble table.

"God help us, not another war! I hope the United States stays out of it," Mother said, flinging her hands about.

Just the word "war" sounded frightening to me, no matter what number it was.

"We'll see," Dad said, lighting up one of his long, brown, King Edward cigars.

I went back to bed and put the thoughts of war far from my mind by picking up my *Air Today* magazine. I was amused to read about the rates a flying circus charged for stunts and tore out the page to show to Glenn the next time I saw him. An article about Mrs. Roosevelt taking flying lessons was inspiring.

My cannery job money was only enough to get in a few hours of practice lessons once a month, since I also had to save for college. Even the bus cost a pretty penny. I calculated how many months it would take me to log my 35 hours for a license, and it seemed so far out of my reach. At least I finally had the 10 hours with Mr. Schelling that I needed to solo the next Saturday. I drifted off to sleep with my clothes on, dreaming I was barrel rolling in a bright yellow Curtiss Jenny.

Saturday came at last. I wore my best Sunday blouse, the peach organdy with the rolled collar, under my old indigo blue coveralls. I grabbed my purse by the top strap and ran for the bus.

When I arrived at the office, I put my purse in a locker and headed toward the hangar. Parked on the side of the tarmac were two Piper Cubs and one slightly bigger plane that I didn't know the name of. Wheel chocks held them steady and several ropes tied them down so the wind wouldn't pick them up. I walked up to one, tracing my hand along the classy, horizontal black stripe that ended in a lightning bolt, contrasting against the bright yellow paint.

Mr. Schelling waved me over. "Hi, Miss Willey, are you ready for your solo?"

"I'm pretty sure, Mr. Schelling." I hid my hands so he wouldn't see them trembling.

"You're a very determined young lady and a fast learner. I think you'll do fine," he said, unfastening the ropes on the Cub.

I approached the yellow Piper Cub slowly, walked around it, and did my preflight inspection. I went over the checklist in my mind. *Any obvious damage to the exterior, any oil or fuel leaks? No. Tires, brakes, propeller – check.* Everything looked good.

Mr. Schelling got in the plane to apply the brakes while I stood at the propeller. I had to stand on my tiptoes to reach the prop, and it took all my strength to pull it through several compressions, enough to get it going. I tossed the wheel chocks off to the side. Ducking under the wing of the Cub, I pulled the tiny metal handle that pushed a side panel down so I could get inside. After I hauled myself into the cockpit, I made sure all the instruments on the control panel were ready for a proper takeoff.

Mr. Schelling hopped out and shouted over the propeller noise, "Good luck!"

Everything checks out fine, I thought, trying to feel confident, even though I was worried I had forgotten something.

I taxied slow and steady down the runway, pushed the throttle forward, began the takeoff roll, and made a nice climb upward. I felt the power of throwing myself happily into the sky, seeing the familiar world from every angle. At first I realized I was holding my breath, and felt again as though I had forgotten something. The plane seemed somehow lighter. Then I laughed. It felt lighter because I was alone for the first time. It was similar to my first experience of getting on the bus without Mother or Dad, but flying far surpassed that small adventure.

I imagined Mr. Schelling lecturing me while I was flying, telling me to "become one with the plane." Just that one phrase boosted my confidence as I ascended and did a smooth S turn. I smiled, wondering what Mr. Schelling would say if I started barrel rolling! I was a free spirit, feeling the movement of the rudder pedals waving within my whole body. I fell in love with the sensation of flying; it was like a powerful thirst I couldn't quench. Pushing forward on the throttle gave me a burst of power. Flying was a magical, visual feast. The lake became a pond. The cows and automobiles became little dots. I was feeling "one with the Cub," so much so that I didn't really want to come down, but knew that I should. I attempted to make a nice descent. Bumping a little on touchdown, I taxied toward the hangar, wiping little beads of sweat from my nose.

Mr. Schelling gave me a wave as I climbed out. "You made a fine descent, but your landing was a bit rough."

"I know. I'll make sure the next solo is better," I answered with certainty.

"I bet it will be." He grinned. "Let's go into the office. I'll sign your log book."

I almost felt like skipping. Flying solo had boosted my confidence.

The next day after church, I changed and headed out

the back door toward Glenn's pasture, ignoring Mother as she shouted, "Violet, where are you going?"

As I hiked through the field, I spotted our dog, Blotchy. His coat was spattered with black and white patches, like a dairy cow. "Here boy," I said, and then whistled his special "come here" whistle. I bent over and let him lick my face, then he followed me across the field.

Glenn was checking the oil on the Jenny. He wore his Sunday white-collared shirt under his brown leather jacket and his dashing barnstormer's white scarf. Just the sight of him stirred up the insides of my body, filling me with exhilaration.

"Glenn, I got to solo and have 10 hours in. Please, let me fly the Jenny." I spoke so fast that spit ran down my face. Embarrassed, I wiped it off with the back of my hand.

"All right, Amelia Junior, climb in and I'll teach you how to make a loop. Now, listen to me carefully before we go up. Make a shallow dive and pick up speed, pull back on the stick, then zoom upward and arch back until you're upside down. Continue down and around to level off near the point of your original climb, then land her. Did you get that?"

"Yes!" I said with confidence as I got into the front cockpit. I knew Glenn had the same controls in the back, and could rescue me at any time.

We made a smooth, shallow dive. I picked up the right amount of speed and, sure enough, was able to do a complete loop. I landed the Jenny gently and waited for the tailskid to make a furrow in the dirt to slow us down. Turning to look behind me, I hoped for a positive response from Glenn.

He gave me his charming smile, with his usual thumbs-up. "That was a magnificent loop, sweetheart. Your flying lessons are paying off, and that was a great landing."

"Thanks! That means a lot to me." My cheeks flushed. Had I heard him right? Did he really call me sweetheart? I glanced over at him. Sure enough, his deep-brown eyes had a look of affection that I had only ever seen in my dad's eyes. A warm, deep glow spread within me.

Leaning over the cockpit, he drew me in like a smooth descent with a kiss.

I pulled away, blushing. "I love doing the loops."

"Are you ready to do a barrel roll?"

"You bet I am!"

"Okay then, first you must gain sufficient speed to get the nose well above the horizon. When you see a point like a smokestack, roll. Never change your altitude and keep your eyes on the point." He demonstrated the technique quite nicely with his hands.

His explanation reminded me of when I saw my friend Polly pirouette on her toes. She would select a point to look at, then turn.

We took off and I said a silent prayer to help me do

the barrel roll. When we were above the town, I spied a smokestack and started the maneuver. Ignoring the droplets of sweat on my forehead, I held my breath and spun around. As soon as I realized I was successful in accomplishing the trick, I was filled with blissful exhilaration. I flew the Jenny back to the field, and made a fabulous descent.

Glenn gave me a look of pride, acknowledging that my first barrel roll was a success. I reached into the pocket of my coveralls and handed him a piece of paper across the cockpit.

"I found the funniest article in my *Air Today* magazine. You've got to read it."

He took the article and read it out loud:

"In 1925, the 13 Black Cats Flying Circus handed out the following flyer advertising the prices for their stunts:

Crash ships (fly into trees, houses, etc.)	*$1,200*
Loop with man on each wing standing up	*$450*
Ship change	*$100*
Upside-down change	*$500*
Fight on upper wing, one man knocked off	*$225*
Upside-down flying with man on landing gear	*$150*
Head-on collision with automobiles	*$250*
Blow up plane in midair, pilot chutes out	*$1,500*

"This is hysterical. Those certainly were the days!" Glenn slapped the side of his pants. "Let's work up a show for today. I have some swell ideas. Can I keep this?" he asked, folding up the flyer.

"Sure. Glad you liked it as much as I did." I loved that we had the flying bug in common. Blotchy was still hanging around, which gave me a great idea. "Let's bring Blotchy up with us. The crowds would love it!" I scratched the dog behind his floppy ears.

"Great idea! I have an extra helmet and goggles we can put on him, but let's tie a rope leash, to keep him secure." Blotchy rolled around in the field as Glenn scratched his stomach affectionately.

The leather cap was loose on Blotchy. I hoped it would stay on, as it was usually skintight on me.

Off we flew to town, hoping the crowds could hear and see Blotchy barking when we flew upside down. I hoped they would be able to see a dog with goggles and a helmet.

High in the air, Glenn dropped out a handful of 100 pennies he had saved up for an event like this. It was fun to be able to leave little presents for the townspeople. I patted Blotchy on the head and he licked my cheek. I was glad he enjoyed flying as much as I did. The breezy air hitting his face made him hang his tongue out, just like he did when we went for a ride in Dad's Model A.

We ended the show with 10 spins in a row. Blotchy barked like all get-out, then got a furious whimpering going, making me feel anxious for him. I was glad it was over as we landed in my back cornfield.

As we climbed out, I hugged Blotchy. "Sorry boy, I forgot to tell you going upside down might be scary."

Glenn stroked Blotchy's fluffy little head. "Good dog, Blotchy. I don't think we should have taken you upside down."

I touched Glenn's scarf, smiling, glad to see this caring side of his personality. "Golly, those stunts gave me quite a thrill. Tell me what we did."

"I did a split S, half roll, quarter roll, snap roll, hammerhead, whip, falling leaf, wingover and a chandelle," he said, counting them off on his fingers.

"You're so talented!" I exclaimed as I took off my helmet and goggles.

"Thanks, you're pretty swell yourself." He leaned over and kissed me.

I heard the sound of my brother, Tommy, on his bicycle. I surely wouldn't want him tattling to Mother, so I turned away from Glenn. Thankfully, he didn't see us kissing. Tommy reached into his newspaper bag and pulled out the can I had found for him to help us during the show.

"I heard barking in the airplane and figured you had Blotchy. I think everyone else heard a dog, too. Almost everyone loved the show. The people who didn't get stung by the pennies picked them off the ground and put them in the can!" Tommy said proudly, rattling around all the coins.

"Oh, no, I didn't think about the pennies hurting anyone! Thanks for helping, Tommy. We couldn't have done it without you," Glenn said. He tousled my brother's hair, which made me smile. Glenn reached inside his pocket and pulled out a very large marble. He tossed it to Tommy. "Here, sport, I'm giving you my best shooter for all your help."

Tommy caught the marble in midair. It was clear, with black in the middle. "Wowee, I've never seen one like this! I bet I could win my next game with this marble." He rolled it around and around in the palm of his hand.

I flashed Glenn my best Shirley Temple smile. Tommy shoved the marble into his pocket, and divided up the money.

"Yippie! I've never had this much money!" Tommy shouted, and took his share home on his bicycle.

"You're quite a go-getter," Glenn said, smiling at me with admiration in his eyes. "Thanks for helping me put on a great show. With your quick learning ability, I think you'll really go places."

"Thanks, but you know, I just want to get my license and fly away from my mother," I said, feeling anxious about seeing her when I got home.

"With your flying fever, it'll happen. I have great news. I found a way to get more money and use my plane at the same time. Postmaster Farley said the Postal Service has been requesting a pilot to deliver and pick up mail in the rural areas. He offered me the job, and I took it." He put the wheel chocks on to keep the Jenny in place.

"Nice, that's right up your alley."

"I'm pretty happy about it. I start on Monday. I won't be seeing you as much, but at least we'll have Sundays together." He reached out for my hand.

"My classes begin soon at San Jose State. I'll be busy, too," I said. "I'll miss our flying adventures together."

I looked at him longingly. We both fell toward each other with a long, passionate kiss.

"You sure taste delicious," he said, stroking my cheek softly.

"No, *you* do!" I answered playfully.

"No, *you* do!" he echoed.

We both started laughing, enjoying our banter.

"Violet, are you there?" I heard mother shouting in the distance.

"Uh-oh, I'd better go." I gave him one last hug and hiked off to my farmhouse, tensely biting the inside of my cheek. When I got there, I crept up the porch steps, nervous about seeing Mother, and whether I'd gotten away with flying with Glenn. I should have told Tommy to keep our adventure a secret.

Chapter Five: Pearl Harbor

"Vi, I've told you many times not to bang the screen door. Hold it before it closes. I have to fix the hinge on it."

"Okay, Dad, sorry," I said, grateful for his patience and the buffer from Mother's scolding.

"Violet, come here, I want to talk to you," Mother said with a look of displeasure on her face.

"What is it?" I said in an overly polite tone as I headed into the kitchen.

"I know you've been up in an airplane with that Glenn boy, showing off all over town, and I don't like it one bit." Her hands were placed firmly on her wide hips.

I was furious with my brother.

I'm going to let him have it as soon as I can find him, I thought. *I can't believe he told!* With a flushed face I said, "Don't worry, he's a skilled pilot. Don't you know his parents, Mr. and Mrs. Conney?"

"You can't kid me, young lady. I know you're trying to sidestep the problem here. It's not a matter of whether I know his parents. I'm talking about safety. It's extremely dangerous what you've been doing, and I'm putting a stop to it immediately. Mrs. Jackson from down the road rang me up and told me all about it. I was so embarrassed." She drummed her fingers on her hips, glaring at me.

"Did you know that the Gates Flying Circus took a million passengers up for joy rides without any serious injuries?" I giggled as I looked out the kitchen window, realizing this tactic probably wouldn't fly.

Dad came in right after I spilled that stupid remark. "Is something wrong?" He scratched the back of his balding head.

"I've had about as much as I can take of Violet's flying shenanigans," Mother said, repinning her tight, grayish-brown rolled bun.

"Dear, didn't you know the barnstormers used to say the greatest danger in flying is starving to death?" He let out a big laugh, rocking on his boots with his hands in his coveralls.

I laughed along with him, but felt the uneasiness in the air once I noticed Mother's horrified look of disgust.

Trying to appease the sticky situation, I said, "That was my last time flying with Glenn. He got a job with the post office and I'll be in school."

Mother removed her hands from her hips and repositioned her bun again. "Praise the Lord. Now, be useful and help me set the table."

As I set out the dinner plates, Tommy came into the dining room with our little brother, Howie, following behind. He gave me a look that said, *I know, I got in trouble, too.* We all sat down and held hands as Dad said grace.

"Lord, help our children do well in school this year and let us pray the war in Europe ends soon. In the name of the Father and the Son and the Holy Ghost." He solemnly crossed himself.

My heart always jumped every time the word "war" was mentioned.

"I hope our country doesn't get involved in fighting this war," Mother said in a worried tone.

"The Lend-Lease program has been put in place so Britain can end it without us," Dad said.

"I hope you're right." Mother cut her meat sharply.

"Please pass the mint jelly," I said, hoping to change the subject as I sliced into a piece of my lamb.

"Here you go, Vi. Do you have enough money for college books?"

"I think I saved up just enough." I mashed up my potatoes, happy to hear Howie belch, keeping the table conversation away from my business.

The next day, I took the bus to San Jose State College. It was only my second time seeing the campus, and I was still astounded by how spread out and huge it was compared to my high school. I saw a few familiar faces, but there were many people I didn't know.

The newness of being at college was quite exciting for

me, but as the month went on I found the classes boring, even though I was getting an A in my science class and B's in the rest.

One day in the hall, I stopped to read a flyer on the bulletin board. The illustration of an airplane caught my eye.

Civilian Pilot Training Program:
Sign up in Brooks Hall, Classroom 207
October 19, 2 PM
$40.00

My hand trembled as I put a finger on the paper. *This will be perfect for me,* I thought. *I can still go to college like Mother wants, and take a flying class. She'd never know! I hope Dad will keep it a secret from her…*

I did fear Mother's tiresome tirade: "A better place to meet a proper beau is in college, not flying a dirty old plane."

Thankfully, I had worked all summer and had earned the $40 for the CPTP class, which was certainly an easier goal than the $500 for private lessons.

That night, I went into the living room to talk to Dad while Mother put away the dinner dishes. He was looking at one of the *Air Today* magazines Uncle Walt bought, and smoking his cigar. I breathed in the smoke, enjoying the familiar, comforting smell as I stood on the circular braided rug that I'd helped Mother make over the years from all our old wool clothing. I circled around one of the braids with my shoe.

"How are your classes going?" he asked, taking a big puff.

"I've been getting A's and B's on all my exams. There's a Civilian Pilot Training Program being offered at college." I looked into the kitchen and saw Mother at the sink, and lowered my voice. "I really want to take it."

"How much does it cost?" He put the magazine down.

"Forty dollars, which is much easier for me to pay for than private lessons. I'd still have enough money for books." I chewed the sides of my cuticles.

"I've heard about the Civilian Pilot Training Program. The president signed a proposal to encourage them so college students could learn to fly. Are you sure you have the extra money?" he said as he tapped the ash of his cigar into a square metal ashtray.

"I've been saving up from the cannery job and I've been helping Tommy with his newspaper route." I rebraided a loose strand of hair.

"Well, honey, I don't know what your mother would say." He tapped his cigar over and over.

I pushed my lips together as I felt my eyes tear up a

bit. "Oh please, Dad, all I can think about is flying. It's the only thing I want to do in my life. My instructor, Mr. Schelling, said that I have a lot of potential."

"I think it's a good idea, Violet, and you've already had some experience. You'll probably pass this college pilot training class easily. I wish I could do it myself." He chuckled, then added, "Maybe we shouldn't mention it to your mother until after you pass it and get your license."

"Thanks for your vote of confidence, Daddy!" I kissed him on his forehead, looked out toward the kitchen, and felt grateful that Mother was nowhere to be seen.

The first day of piloting class was energizing. I glanced around the classroom. There were mostly boys with just a sprinkling of girls. The fellas were handsome, but not as good-looking as my Glenn. I began to daydream, then I realized the teacher was talking. I straightened up and listened, wanting to take it all in.

"Welcome, class, to the first civilian training program at San Jose State," said Mr. Reid. "We can thank the great President Roosevelt for signing a proposal to provide pilot training to 20,000 college students around the nation. Our program includes supplying one Piper J-3 Cub for every 10 students. You will have 72 hours of ground school followed by 35 hours of flight training. At our college we're very proud to offer this class, but you may hear some controversy. In the newspaper there was an article saying it was a New Deal pork-barrel waste of tax dollars. I just wanted to make you aware of this, since the college vehemently defends this course, as it will provide a large base of trained pilots in case we become involved in the war. Are there any questions so far?" Mr. Reid loosened his tie in the stuffy classroom.

I became quite stirred up when he said we'd be flying Piper Cubs, since I'd already passed a solo in one. I felt this put me a step ahead.

Mother allowed me to invite Glenn over to Sunday dinner. I knew she didn't approve of airplane pilots very much, but I could tell that since Glenn worked for the post office now and was a member of our church, she thought he was acceptable.

"How's your mail delivery coming along, Glenn?" Mother said, warming up to his presence. "Pass the roast beef, Tommy."

"It's been very productive, Mrs. Willey," he said, as he sipped from his tall glass of milk. "I've been delivering mail six days a week and make $2.21 a mile."

"Oh, my," exclaimed Mother. "That's a good amount of money. Howie, stop that gulping noise."

Dad gave Howie a stern look, then asked Glenn, "Do you also pick up mail in other towns?"

Glenn politely wiped his mouth with our best

monogrammed cloth napkins before speaking. "Yes, sir, the technique is called 'skyhooking.' Many of the small towns don't have airports for me to land, so the outgoing mail is put in a special weighted rubber canister that hangs on a rope suspended between a pair of 15-foot-high posts."

"That's ingenious, but how do you get the mail up into the air?"

"I put a grappling hook on the tail of my airplane and my assistant reels it in," Glenn said proudly.

"Sounds like your stunt pilot skills have come in handy," Dad said, and then shot Howie another look for burping.

"That's right, sir, it does take a little bit of acrobatic skill to do the skyhooking." He grinned.

It was wonderful listening to Dad and Glenn talk and I glanced at them warmly.

The mood changed as Mother said, "It seems like a very dangerous job to me." She put on her cross face, causing immediate silence at the table.

I walked Glenn out the door onto the front porch. "Sorry my mother is so nasty."

"She means well." He looked around and kissed me goodnight.

I kissed him back. I said goodbye, only to see Mother looking toward us through the door.

The semester went by fast once I started taking the CPTP classes. After I got off the bus from college one day, I ran inside the barn looking for Dad.

"Look Dad, here it is!" I proudly waved my pilot's license at his surprised face. I was the first in the class to get my license before the semester was over, because I had taken private lessons.

Dad scanned it, seeing the documented hours of flying time recorded.

"By golly, girl, you did it. My only daughter, flying in the sky like Amelia Earhart, and you don't even know how to drive an automobile! I did end up telling your mother about your pilot classes, but let's not mention your license, just to keep the peace. My little Vi-Vi's all grown up now. I'm very proud of you!" He embraced me tightly.

"Thanks for your moral support, Dad, and don't fret. I'll just talk to Mother about all my other classes."

The following day I was in my room getting on my church clothes while Mother made sure my brothers were cleaned up. I carefully selected a dress that Glenn might like. I couldn't wait to tell Glenn about getting my pilot's license. I smelled Dad's cigar and opened my door a crack since I knew he always listened to the Zenith before church.

"This is an emergency news bulletin. The Japanese have attacked Pearl Harbor, Hawaii, by air!"

The radio announcer sounded almost hysterical. I stepped outside my room and heard him repeat:

"The Japanese have bombed Pearl Harbor! The great Pearl Harbor Naval base was just attacked by dive-bombing planes bearing the rising sun insignia of Japan. The first attack began at 7:33 A.M. and several more attacks have followed. The Japanese strike has inflicted untold damage on the Naval base and on the city itself. Aerial dogfights have raged in the skies over Honolulu as American warplanes have risen to give battle to the Japanese invaders."

Bombing of Pearl Harbor

Mother hurried in just as the announcer said the word, "bombing" on the radio. "Harry, what are they talking about?"

"The Japanese have bombed Pearl Harbor, Hawaii."

"God save us! How are we going to survive this?" Mother cried, shaking her apron.

"It's okay, dear, our country has enough manpower to help us with this situation. I only wish I was young enough to join the service. Too bad our boys aren't older." He snubbed out his King Edward.

Mother's eyes narrowed. "It's time to go to church. We'll just make the last Mass. God knows we sure have a lot to pray about now. Tommy, Howie, are you ready? Get into the car with your sister," she said sternly.

After church, I stood with Glenn on the steps while we listened to our parents talking.

"It's a damn shock about the bombing in our own territory of Hawaii," Mr. Conney said, solemnly tucking in his shirt over his large belly.

"This might be the start of our involvement in the war, I'm sorry to say," Dad replied.

Mother and Mrs. Conney whispered to each other, shaking their heads.

I had never seen Glenn look so glum. "We all better take this bombing seriously."

"I just hate the idea of war," I said, chewing one of my fingernails.

"No one likes the concept of war and our country has been avoiding it, but now it's too near and *not* just in Europe anymore."

"Time to go, Violet," Mother called from the bottom of the church steps, grabbing Tommy's and Howie's hands firmly as she headed toward the car.

Glenn looked at my sad eyes, kissed me on the cheek, and said, "See you next Sunday. Hope you do well in school." He stared up toward the sky. The dark, rainy clouds of winter were beginning to form. Then he followed his parents out into the street.

I could tell he was trying to reassure me, but his thoughts seemed to be elsewhere.

It was hard to go to school the next day, listening to all the students talking about Pearl Harbor. I hadn't even heard of the place before. I felt numb.

That night, Dad went into the living room and glued himself to the radio. Interrupting my studies, I listened to President Roosevelt's booming, articulate voice from the Zenith, and opened my door to listen.

"Yesterday, December 7th, 1941 – a date which will live in infamy – the United States of America was suddenly and deliberately attacked by naval and air forces of the Empire of Japan."

Dazed, I walked into the living room, and slumped on the red-and-green paisley chair on the other side of the radio. Dad gravely nodded as we listened to the end of the president's address to the nation:

"I ask that Congress declare that since the unprovoked and dastardly attack by Japan on Sunday, December 7th, 1941, a state of war has existed between the United States and the

Japanese Empire."

"Thank the Good Lord we have such a competent president in office," Dad said.

I felt confused about the announcement of war, and retreated into my room as Kate Smith ended the broadcast singing "God Bless America."

Two days after hearing the devastating news of the war, I got off the bus and there was Glenn, waiting for me. He looked very handsome in his postal uniform. I was surprised to see him, since he was usually too busy with his mail delivery route to see me midweek.

Glenn gathered me in his arms, held me close, and with a serious look on his face said, "I've decided to join up. I don't want this war to end up in our country. When I saw the poster in town with a picture of a fighter plane saying, 'Be a Marine Flyer,' I signed up right away."

I squeezed him tighter and pleaded, "I don't want you to go, but I know our country needs you more than I do. The war is all that Dad's been talking about." Tears formed in my eyes.

"Sweets, you're only 19. I don't expect you to wait for me. With your ambition and brains, you'll do great in college. I don't have the smarts like you do; I'd rather join up to serve my country than struggle through college like I did in high school." He kissed me behind my ear and put his strong hands on my waist.

"I'll wait for you, Glenn. You've taught me so many things about flying, and you mean everything to me." Though I had never been the one to initiate affection, I kissed him passionately. Now, the excitement of getting my pilot's license seemed too inconsequential to even mention. I clung to his muscular arm, wondering what my life would be like without him.

Chapter Six: Women Airforce Service Pilots

After Glenn left for the service in January, I was obsessed with getting the mail. Every day after school I went into the house without any greeting and asked Mother, "Is there a letter for me?" Most of the time there was nothing. I kept myself busy by challenging myself to get an A in English, which was my hardest subject. For some reason, math and science came easily to me.

After a few weeks, which felt more like months, the answer to my daily question was finally, "On the table, dear."

Thank Heaven! There was a letter from Glenn. I immediately tore it open.

Dearest Violet:

I'm finishing up with basic training and will be sent shortly on a flying mission. My experience with airplanes helped me pass the tests to join a squadron.

The Marine Corps is a tough outfit to be in, but I am happy to say it is the most superior branch of the service. I will do whatever it takes to help win this dreadful war.

How is college? I heard all flying has ceased on the West Coast since the Pearl Harbor incident. I bet it's driving you nuts not being up in the air where you're always the happiest.

Sometimes I daydream about us settling down to raise a family. I'm hoping you share the same wish as me. I miss you sorely and think of you whenever my mind has time to wander.

What do you say about getting hitched on my first leave? Well, honey, must sign off for now.

All my love, Glenn

I read his letter over and over, love filling me every time. When I closed my eyes I could feel his thick, black hair between my fingers, and remembered his long, passionate kisses. I realized what I missed most about him was his smell. It was different than Dad's. He didn't actually sweat too much since he was a pilot, not a farmer. His scent was all his own and whenever we sat close, I breathed him in as deeply as possible. Just the thought of his sweet smell filled me with an animalistic passion. Oh, how I missed him! The thought of marriage and having his baby made me crave him more. Anxiety crept in as I thought about him being in the Marines. I knew his job as a combat pilot was dangerous, and I silently said a prayer for his safety.

On campus one day, I read in the local newspaper:

Wanted: Women to deliver planes for the Army, Civil Service status, trained by military personnel.

Minimum age: 18-28 years old

Must be at least: 5'2", 120 pounds

High School diploma

Private or commercial pilot's license, minimum 35 hrs.

Pay: $3,000 a year.

Physical exam required, send letter with qualifications to:

Jacqueline Cochran, Director, Women Airforce Service Pilots, Avenger Field, Sweetwater, Texas

Release a man flyer for combat duty.

My heart soared with excitement, followed by my brain. This was it! This could be my fate. If I could join the Service Pilots, my life would really start to head in the right direction. I missed flying dreadfully since all the airports had been closed after the bombing of Pearl Harbor. My only worry now was to get Mom and Dad's permission to join, since I was only 19. I held my cross tightly between my fingers, praying.

When the bus home from college reached my stop, I got off and ran toward the barn to avoid the farmhouse, as well as Mother. I found Dad under the hood, fiddling with his Model A.

"Dad, look at this newspaper ad," I said, waving it in

the air.

He poked his head out from the car and scanned the paper. "Hummm. I know how much you've been itching to fly since the closure of the West Coast to flying, but this job sounds dangerous. I don't think your mother will go for it."

"We need to tell her I won't be near any fighting and the country needs all the people it can get to win this war. Besides, I wouldn't even be involved in combat and I'd only be delivering planes to the Army men in the States. Please, Dad," I begged.

"We'll see." He stuck his head under the hood.

"Dad, please!"

He put his wrench down and leaned over to look at me. "Your cousin Emma just joined the Women's Army and your mother approves. I'll see if I can convince her. You are a girl, which makes it harder. I wish your brothers were older." He stuck his head back under the hood.

Seeing that the discussion had ended, I over-cheerfully said, "Thanks Dad, I'd better go help in the kitchen."

Dad got back to his tinkering as I walked down the straw path toward the farmhouse.

Mother was sweeping the kitchen floor. I saw a pile of freshly picked carrots on the counter, and scrubbed them under the faucet. I mentioned to her about Emma joining the service.

"She has a very important job working for the colonel and the whole family is very proud of her," my mother said.

"Do you have Emma's address? I'd love to write to her."

"I'll get it for you after dinner."

"I'll set the table after I get some studying done," I offered.

Mother smiled at me. "Now that you're older, your studies should come first."

In my room, I jotted off a letter to Emma.

Dear Cousin Emma:

How is Army life? I hope to join the Women Airforce Service Pilots. It's not part of the Army, it's actually Civil Service.

I got my private license and all I want to do is fly. Since Pearl Harbor, the airports are closed to all nonmilitary flying; this way the Armed Forces can keep a close watch on all the planes coming into the United States, making it harder for an enemy plane to sneak in and attack. I haven't left the ground in ages. I am glad you joined the Army, as it allows Mother to see that women are really needed in the service.

I hope and pray I will have the opportunity to fly once again, as well as to be able to serve my country.

Please write back soon and tell me what Army life is like for women. —Your cuz, Violet

After sealing the letter to Emma, I wrote to the Women Airforce Service Pilots, requesting an application.

Several weeks later, I asked Mother, "Any mail for me?"

"Violet, every day you come home from school and ask me this. I never even get a simple hello. What are you looking for in the mail, anyway?" she said in a suspicious voice.

"Sorry, but I'm hoping for a letter from Glenn or Emma."

"The mail's on the table in the living room," she answered curtly.

There, in the middle of the oak dining table, was a large, official-looking envelope. I tore it open. Inside was the application and a form requesting parental permission. Taking it with me to the back orchard, I went to find Dad. Blotchy ran beside me. I bent down and let him lick my face. "It's okay boy, Dad's on my side, he'll get Mother to sign." I playfully wiggled his long, multicolored tail. Playing with Blotchy soothed me.

I saw Dad and called through the orchard, "I got the Service Pilot application in the mail today!"

"Already?" he asked.

"There's a permission form I need signed." Nervous, I pulled leaves off one of the branches.

"Leave that alone." He pruned a slender peach tree branch in half, then bent down and threw the cutting in a pile. "I'll try to talk to your mother tonight. Go inside and help her with the chores."

I handed him the paperwork. "Thanks Dad, you're the best!" Memories of my first plane ride with him came rushing at me, making me feel hopeful about the future. I skipped back home and buttered mother up the best I could.

That night after dinner, I heard Mother and Dad in the midst of a heated conversation in the kitchen. With apprehension, I opened my door to overhear the conversation and peered out.

"I hope signing that paper doesn't put our only daughter in danger," Mother said. Her tone sounded more worried than angry.

"Martha, even your own niece has joined up," Dad said, hooking his thumbs in the straps of his overalls.

"Typing is not the same as flying!" I saw her gnawing on her lip, then turn to resume her ironing.

I stepped back into my bedroom and closed the door. I picked up my grandmother's old handheld mirror, fashioned my pigtails in the back with a clip, and wondered how I would wear my hair in the Army. I saluted at my reflection, saying, "Flying, here I come!"

One day, while riding home from college, I gazed out the window at the pastures going by and wondered if I would ever get a letter from the Army Airforces. I had been waiting for nearly three weeks.

When I got home, I went into the kitchen and breathed in deeply. "That blackberry pie smells marvelous."

"Thanks, dear," Mother said.

"Any mail for me?" I timidly asked.

With a serious voice she said, "There's a telegram on the dining room table. You know, we don't always see eye to eye on everything, but you're my only daughter and I do worry about your future." She looked at me with a sadness I had never seen before, but before I could say anything, she turned her back on me to check on the pie.

I dashed into the dining room to read the telegram.

WESTERN UNION

VIOLET J WILLEY

207 MOUNTAIN VIEW ROAD, SJ

REPORT TO RICE HOTEL, HOUSTON, TEXAS ON 9 JUNE
NORTH BALCONY ADJOINING USO LOUNGE AT 1045 AM FOR
PHYSICAL EXAM.

COME AT OWN EXPENSE. BRING FLIGHT RECORDS.
ACKNOWLEDGE RECEIPT OF TELEGRAM IMMEDIATELY, LETTER
TO FOLLOW.

GENERAL HENRY H. ARNOLD, AAF

JACQUELINE COCHRAN, AIR TRAINING COMMAND

"My application was accepted!" I shouted, doing an elated jig into the kitchen.

Mother adjusted her apron before looking up at me. "You're too young to go off to war. I'd rather you finished your education. "

"I'm not going off to war, Mother. The Women Airforce Service Pilots just deliver planes from the factories to the bases, and only in the United States — not even overseas." I took a breath. "I know you're worried about me, but this is an opportunity for me to serve my country." I held my head up high and looked directly into her sad green eyes.

She answered very softly, "I can't help fearing for your life in those dangerous airplanes. Besides, I thought you had intentions with Glenn." She retied that darned apron once again.

"The WASPs do take married women, and you might as well accept the fact that I care more about flying than college. You know, before I can ferry a plane I have to pass six months of ground school." I crossed my arms in front of my waist defensively.

"You'll be going to school?" she said, surprising me with a smile.

"I'll be taking classes in meteorology, Morse code, mechanics and lots of other subjects." I relaxed my hands to my sides.

"Help me shuck this corn while it's still fresh," she said, changing the subject.

The following letter came the next day:

```
Women Airforce Service Pilots

Avenger Field

Sweetwater, Texas
```

Bring such street clothing you deem desirable, together with funds for living expenses for 30 days. Provisions have been made for your employment on Civil Service status at the rate of $150 a month during your satisfactory pursuance of flying instruction under Army control. Upon completion of Army instruction and if physically qualified, you will be eligible for employment as a utility pilot.

Jacqueline Cochran, Air Training Command

Between studies the following week, I got a chance to write Glenn, telling him the good news.

Darling:

I am joining the Women Airforce Service Pilots. I have caught your fever and also wish to be of service to our country. My other selfish reason, of course, is the need to be in the sky!

Your letter took my breath away and I do want to get hitched on your first leave!

Can you believe the town is holding a parade for me before I go into the service? I feel very anxious about this because I have not really been accepted yet. I still have to pass the physical and interview. It seems that everyone in town is excited to see a girl join up.

I check the mail every day and wish you would write more often. I miss you and worry about you.

All my love, Violet

Chapter Seven: A Physical and an Interview

"Violet, Martha, time to go, the whole town is waiting for us!" Dad hollered.

I got into our car and squished in the back between Howie and Tommy to keep them from fighting. I felt eager and anxious all at the same time. My nervousness was not due to the parade in my honor; rather, it was anxiety about the upcoming physical exam. I was an inch short on the height and five pounds shy on the weight. All this fuss was being made over me, and I hadn't been officially accepted yet. Glenn hadn't received this much attention when he joined the Marines. Dad said I was being honored because I was one of the first girls in town to join the service.

After Dad parked the car, Tommy and Howie got out and joined the parade. They marched by, holding handmade banners that read, "Good Luck, Violet. Fly For Our Troops!" I waved happily from the church steps. The high school band went by, playing Sousa's "Stars and Stripes Forever."

As I watched the parade, I reflected on a squabble I'd had with Mother just before the event. She had taken me aside with tears in her eyes and said, "I know your heart is set on this flying escapade, and if it wasn't for your father's strong will, I'd never have let you join up."

I had argued, "Even Cousin Emma has enlisted."

Mother answered, "Emma is much older than you. Besides, she's just a secretary in the Army and is not flying around in risky airplanes."

My fatigue at bickering with Mother over flying gave me the incentive to move away and join the WASPs. I tried to mention ground school as often as possible, as it seemed to soften her up some.

Once the short parade was over, Mother, Dad and I went to the church hall. There was a wonderful array of food spread out on two long tables. I was about to eat another piece of pie to aid my underweight problem when I noticed Glenn's parents. I waved to them, happy to see my beau's family.

"Congratulations, Violet. It's very honorable of you to serve our country," Mr. Conney said, adjusting his tie. He wore quite an expensive-looking black tailored suit.

"Thanks. Have you heard from Glenn?" I added.

"We got a letter. He's on a mission on a small island called Wake," he said with a proud smile.

Mrs. Conney put down her teacup. "He wrote that he's intending to marry you on his first leave. Is this true?"

"The letter I got from him did include a proposal." I blushed. "I wrote back and said yes."

"We'll be pleased to have you as our daughter." Mr. Conney grinned, then dabbed the pie crumbs from his shirt with his handkerchief.

My cheeks flushed as Mrs. Conney gave me a little hug.

"Glenn has influenced my life a great deal. I think our marriage would be a very compatible union," I said, trying to sound mature to gain the Conneys' approval.

That night, worry dominated my mind rather than sleep. My feelings were mixed up and rolling around in my stomach. Of course, my overeating added to the bubbling. The attention from the townspeople was inspiring, but I still had to pass the physical. I could fudge the height problem by peeling off the heels of old shoes and gluing them on top of my new ones. This would add the two inches I needed that the service required to reach the airplane's pedals. But, I was still five pounds underweight. Thank goodness there had been a lot to eat at the potluck! I tried to lie still, keeping my eyes closed with the hope that just resting would help calm my mind in place of sleep.

Light eventually seeped into my room. I gave up and got out of bed. I glanced at my alarm clock and wasn't surprised to see it was much too early to rouse my family to go to the train station. I yawned and stretched, grateful for the rest I had gotten, even though my eyes felt a bit fuzzy. In the bathroom, I ran a washrag over my face. My confidence in my upcoming future waxed and waned. I had never been out of my town, or even on a train for that matter. I had already packed the only suitcase we owned, and had nothing to do except lie awake waiting for my family to stir.

After what seemed an eternity, we arrived at the train station. Dad had his arm around Mother, while keeping a close eye on the boys. Mother held a small, long white box in her hands. I looked at it, wondering what it could possibly be.

"I want you to have these family pearls, dear. I hope they'll bring you good luck in the airplanes."

I was astonished at this gesture. It made me aware that, despite all our disagreements, Mother really did love me.

Swallowing hard and blinking, I opened the box and choked out, "Thanks, they're beautiful." I tearfully put on the gleaming, iridescent pearls. Mother clasped the back of them for me.

Touching my shoulder, she said, "Make sure you don't lose them, they were my mother's and have been in the family a long time."

This remark was typical. She always ruined any special moments we had with nagging. I sighed, mumbling, "Don't worry, I'll keep them safe." I rolled each round, silky ball between my fingers.

Dad came up to me, his eyes moist. "I'm very proud of you and pleased that someone in our family can help the war effort. Take care of yourself and write as often as you can." He held me firmly, giving me a gentle kiss on my wet cheek.

I went up the metal steps into the train, found a seat, and waved out the window. Unable to fight back my tears, I let them drip down my cheeks as I sucked on one of my braids, slipping into a bad habit from childhood.

Sitting uncomfortably on my suitcase, I looked around at all the uniformed soldiers that occupied the other available seats. This sight brought back the reality of a war going on. I got out the newspaper and buried my face in it. I silently cried, both from the anxiety of unknown events ahead of me, and because I was leaving my family for the first time in my life. The weight of the pearl necklace around my neck gave me a sense of calm. I knew that Mother had given it to me at the last minute as a peace offering. This helped alleviate some of the strain between us.

My old optimism slowly returned, especially after reading a newspaper article on airplane production:

SAN JOSE MERCURY

February 19, 1943

Aircraft production has soared from 19,000 planes to 48,000 in just one year. Thousands of airplanes need to be moved from factories to air bases and for shipment overseas. With male pilots being sent into combat duty, there is a severe shortage of pilots at home.

I got out a letter from my cousin Emma that I had been saving to pass the time on the way to Houston for my physical exam.

Dear Cousin Violet:

I can't believe you are old enough to join the WASPs! I've been hearing all about this part of the service. I'm rooting for you, kid, and hope you make it!

South Carolina is pretty hot, but I try to get in a swim as often as possible, when I am not typing for the colonel.

Enclosed is an article from our base newsletter.

Who knows, cuz, maybe you'll be able to fly out to see me sometime!

Love, Emma

COLUMBIA ARMY BASE NEWS

Women Airforce Service Pilots

Jacqueline Cochran, "that famous rags-to-riches gal," has talked the Army Airforces into accepting women ferry pilots.

She is known as the "First Lady of Flight" and has achieved more "firsts" in aviation history than any other person, man or woman. Mrs. Cochran was the first woman to ferry a bomber across the Atlantic to England.

With the president and Mrs. Roosevelt's backing, women pilots are a secret weapon waiting to be used.

General Henry H. Arnold, Chief of the Air Corps, told the press that the WASPs do not have military status yet, but with Jacqueline Cochran's ambition it may happen in the near future. Mrs. Cochran has set up a base at Avenger Field, Sweetwater, Texas. It is ideal for training with its wide-open, dry, and isolated location.

Putting the letter in the pocket of my skirt, I reflected on what a valuable asset I would be and reassured myself that I was surely doing the right thing.

Quite a few soldiers got off the train at Fort Huachuca, Arizona, enabling me to find a quiet seat where I could doze off. I needed the sleep. It would take several days to get to Texas. I felt a little lonely, since there was no one to talk to, but my silence gave me a sense of calm to prepare myself mentally for what lay ahead.

Several long, tiring days later, the conductor hollered, "Houston!"

I grabbed the worn, brown leather handle of my secondhand suitcase and got off the train. As I wandered around the shadows of the tall buildings of the city, I found a bus stop and just stood there. I was too intimidated and overwhelmed to ask for directions. A bus eventually came. I got on it and asked for the Rice Hotel. The bus driver pointed to the other side of the street, then yelled, "Next!" to the people behind me. I backed down the steps saying, "Excuse me," to a large-breasted woman with groceries in her arms. I had to walk a block just to get to the signal light in order to cross. I was glad the interview wasn't until tomorrow. All of this traveling had exhausted me, and I wasn't at my best.

As I waited at the bus stop, I noticed a full-figured, good-looking Negro girl around my age. I glanced at her as she saw me, and gave her a friendly smile. She was the first Negro I had ever seen in person, and I tried to look her over without her noticing. Her color was very beautiful, dark, and creamy. I found her hair very strange — a tight, wiry mass of black. She caught me glancing at her again, and I put on the nicest face possible. Her teeth were the shiniest white and contrasted against her skin. She smiled back at me, catching my rude stare.

A half hour later a bus came with a sign on it that read *Rice Hotel*. It was packed with quite an assortment of people. The Negro girl got onboard. A seat next to me was the only one available on the crowded bus, but she passed me by and headed toward the back to stand. I almost turned around to shout that there was a place next to me available, when I remembered the segregation laws in the South. *How sad*, I thought. *She could probably use a friend to sit with.*

"Rice Hotel," the bus driver shouted some minutes later.

I got off and stood gaping at the fancy building ornamented with stone gargoyles. It certainly was the grandest hotel I had ever laid my eyes on. Feeling someone come up behind me, I turned to find the girl from the bus.

"Hi, I'm Violet Willey," I said, holding out an awkward hand.

"Name's Esther Calhoun," she said with an accent I had never heard before.

"Are you headed into the Rice Hotel?" I asked.

"I sure enough am, miss," she replied, looking down at the street.

She said nothing more. I wondered if she was also here for the physical to join the WASPs. I felt too shy to ask at first, but then I found the courage to ask her.

"I sure enough am, miss," she replied once again.

"So am I. How about we share a room together?" I smiled brightly.

"That'll be just fine," Esther answered.

Her face was expressionless and I couldn't really tell what she was thinking. Esther felt around in her worn purse and gave me some money.

"I'll make sure you get the change back if the room costs less," I said.

Esther nodded.

We entered a sparkling lobby that was decorated with high-backed, dark-red velvet chairs. The chandeliers adorning the tall ceiling were dripping with long rows of exquisite crystals. The elegance of the hotel startled me so much that I had trouble seeing where the registration desk was. Looking out toward the end of the grand room,

I saw the main inquiry counter.

"Looks like we check in here," I said to Esther.

She stayed behind me as I asked the clerk for a hotel room for two. He wore a uniform outlined in gold-braided piping. The clerk took my money and put two keys down on the counter.

A couple next to me impatiently asked, "Are there any rooms with a view?"

Thank goodness this hotel is busy and people won't suspect that Esther and I are sharing a room, I thought. Turning back toward Esther with a grin, I was happy to have gotten away with getting two keys. Esther kept her eyes cast down at the floor and followed behind me as we headed to the elevator.

The upward motion of the elevator caused a funny sensation in my belly that reminded me of a barrel roll in the Jenny. I felt a twinge of homesickness and longed for my Glenn. I looked over at Esther, who still had a blank look on her face as she stared at the numbers going by.

After settling into our room, I handed Esther her change. She shyly said, "Thank you, miss."

My eyes widened as Esther called me "miss" once more. I had never in my life been called "miss."

"How'd y'all learn to fly?" she asked in a warmer tone.

Just the word "fly" got me into a conversational mood. "The first time I went up in a Curtiss Jenny was when

I was seven. I rode with my dad, after he spotted a barnstormer flying over our farmhouse." I smoothed out the lacy bedspread that covered one of the beds and sat down, smiling as I recalled the memory.

"Well, I'll be. The first time I went up was also in a Jenny. I flew with the famous aviatrix, Bessie Coleman; she was the first Negro woman barnstormer in '25. I got my pilot's license at her flying school. If it hadn't been for Bessie, I would've never dreamed of signing up for the WASPs." Esther looked out the window when she spoke, avoiding eye contact with me.

Her earlier blunt sentences had made me feel uncomfortable, but I was delighted to hear about her passion for flying.

"I've heard about Bessie Coleman," I said.

"You have?" Esther said with surprise.

"I've read everything I could get my hands on about barnstorming. I was born too late to put on shows like there used to be, but my fiancé and I used to do little performances for our town." I surprised myself when the word *fiancé* slipped out. My cheeks reddened. "Where are you from, Esther? I've never heard an accent like yours before." I slipped off my heels and stretched out on the big comfy bed.

"Florida. If it wasn't for Bessie sponsoring me, I would've never been able to get my pilot's license or make it to Texas." Esther's dark-brown eyes shone as they connected with mine.

71

"Are you worried about the physical?"

"I'm more nervous about passing the interview." Esther examined the hotel room's carpet. We both got lost in our own thoughts.

The physical exam was held in the lower level of the hotel. There seemed to be thousands of men in all states of undress, causing my heart to beat faster. The few women that were there wore a variety of clothing. Some wore cowboy boots, while others were in three-piece tailored suits with high heels. I felt out of place as I pulled at my wrinkled plaid skirt and pinned back my pigtails, trying to look older. Concerned about my newly fashioned double-heeled shoes, I bowed my head and prayed silently: *Please Lord, help me pass the physical; protect and surround me.* I crossed myself.

When it was my turn to stand on the scale, I felt nauseated when the Army flight surgeon slid the bar. "You barely make the weight and sure are a skinny little thing," he said, waving his clipboard.

I blushed and lied, "I've been dieting for my boyfriend."

"Take your shoes off and stand against the measuring stick on the wall." He pointed.

Oh no, I thought, *how stupid of me!* Of course they didn't measure you with your shoes on. I reluctantly took off my double-glued loafer heels and stood as high as I could against the wall.

"Hmm," he muttered, narrowing his eyes at me. "I'm very reluctant to sign your physical. You scarcely made the height or weight, and aren't even 21. You know, young lady, I don't think women should be in the military." He rubbed his bald head and glared at me.

My words tumbled from my mouth. "Sir, the WASPs are not involved in combat. They help our men by ferrying aircraft from the factories to the bases so they can get overseas faster to fight."

The doctor frowned and shook his head. All that mattered to me was that he agreed to sign the physical form.

"Thanks, sir," I said quietly, holding my hand out for the paper. It was the first of hundreds of "sirs" I would use in the days to come.

I had only flown the minimum required 35 hours, was 19 years old, and felt like I was barely making it. Next, I had to pass the interview with the renowned Jacqueline Cochran. Beads of sweat formed on my upper lip as I entered the interview room.

Inside were eight jittery girls, including Esther, waiting for Mrs. Cochran to show up.

"Violet Willey," Director Cochran called from her office. The door was wide open and left no privacy.

73

With butterflies in my stomach, I apprehensively walked into the office. As I sat face to face with the legendary aviatrix, I mustered up courage from the bottom of my soul and focused on my great ability to fly. She looked quite refined in her expensive black-and-white striped, worsted wool suit. It was tailored like a man's with wide lapels, and big black buttons. Her satin blouse added a soft feminine flavor to her outfit, along with her dainty diamond earrings, which sparkled when she talked. Her lips were voluptuous, like a Hollywood movie star's, but then maybe it was the dark-red color that made them appear that way.

"Here's my pilot's license and logbook, Director," I said, presenting them to her, my hand shaking.

She scanned them over. "Tell me, Miss Willey, why do you want to fly for the United States Army?"

"I'm a fast learner, have a passion for flying, and I want to serve my country," I said, pulling at my skirt hem.

Director Cochran jotted something in her notebook, handed back my records, and looked past me. "Next."

I anxiously slipped back to the waiting room. When I saw Esther get up to be interviewed, I decided to sit back down close to the office.

I saw Esther's hand tremble as she presented her logbook to Director Cochran.

"I see you attended Bessie Coleman's Flying School," Mrs. Cochran said with admiration in her voice.

"Yes, ma'am," Esther said. She held her hands squeezed together on her lap.

"Miss Calhoun, you're qualified to join the Service Pilots, but I must tell you, we're not set up to have Negroes. We'd have to have separate barracks and dining facilities. The main problem is that this job requires ferrying planes all over the States, and I would be very apprehensive about your safety, or even being able to get hotel rooms between bases. I have great respect for your instructor, Miss Coleman. Please give her my regards, but I'm sorry to say I cannot accept you. If only we were not in a time of forced segregation, which I do not support, I'd welcome you into our service. I'm truly sorry and wish you luck, Miss Calhoun." Mrs. Cochran held out her hand.

"Thanks, ma'am." Esther returned her handshake, then briskly walked past me before I could talk to her.

I got up, hurried to the elevator, and impatiently waited in the hallway for it to stop. The hotel had so many floors that the passing of the lighted numbers seemed to take forever. At last, I heard the ding and the doors opened, and I dashed inside. Unfortunately, the elevator stopped at every floor before it finally reached mine. I got off, and dashed quickly down the hall into our room, hoping to comfort my new friend. Esther's bed appeared as if no one had ever slept there, while mine was a tangled mess. I felt saddened and eerie. It was as though she never really existed.

I flopped on my bed, feeling sad for the girl who had

gotten her pilot's license, but did not get a chance to fly simply because of her skin color. This sour mood wrapped itself around me. Maybe I wouldn't make it, either. Maybe I didn't have enough hours. Maybe the physician wrote down that I didn't weigh enough. Did I even have enough money to make it on the bus to Sweetwater if I did get accepted? Dad said I could borrow some, but I knew Mother would argue with him over this. All these worries overwhelmed me.

After a stomach-churning, sleepless night, a knock came at my door. I opened it just enough to peek out to see a blue-capped messenger. He presented me with a notice.

```
Report at once: Avenger Field, Sweetwater, Texas
        Women Airforce Service Pilots.
         General Henry H. Arnold, AAF
    Jacqueline Cochran, Commanding Officer
```

I grasped the paper with excitement, wishing I could share this news with Glenn. He would be very proud of me! I hadn't heard from him in months. I knew he was most likely too busy with a mission to write. I hoped he still cared for me.

I took a shower. My bad mood washed away down the drain with the soap bubbles. I put on my best navy pleated church dress and my not-so-white gloves. On my head I fashioned my dark-brown tam and pulled my braids back with a barrette. This was the only store-bought dress I owned. I had saved enough money last year to order it out of the Sears catalog. All my other dresses Mother had helped me sew. Turning about in front of the hotel's lovely, gold-framed mirror, I was satisfied with my appearance. I took the elevator down to the front desk to turn in my key, and inquired how to get to Sweetwater. Once in the lobby, I looked for Esther, but there were only white folks milling about. I silently bowed my head, saying a prayer for good fortune to come her way.

Chapter Eight: Basic Training

The train ride to the base lulled me to sleep with its *clickety clack, clickety clack.* At least this time it was not crowded with troops, and I found a seat right away. A few hours later, I transferred to a bus. The ride was very dusty through the barren countryside. I passed the time by writing a letter to Glenn.

Dear Honey:

I am proud to say, I passed my physical and interview. I am on my way to Sweetwater. Flying, here I come, at last!

"Hey, miss, we're at Avenger Field," the jovial bus driver shouted back toward where I sat.

I tucked the unfinished letter into my purse, rose from my seat, and looked out the bus door to the huge entryway to the base. *Aviation Enterprises LTD,* it said in bold white letters. Above it, standing on a miniature globe, was a strange-looking cartoon character with aviation goggles and wings. I gave the bus driver a little wave, got off, then walked down the dirt roadway, dragging my heavy suitcase along behind me.

Full of anxiety, I hoped the first building I came to was the right one. As I entered, I saw a room full of girls chatting.

"Is this the administration building?" I asked a tall gal on my right.

"Yeah, you made it, now hush up. The one and only Jacqueline Cochran is about to speak," the brash girl replied.

The gorgeous Director Cochran stood before us. She wore a spectacular outfit; far more glamorous than the one I had seen during my interview. It was a two-piece, cocoa-colored rayon crepe suit. She accented it with black gabardine, and open-toe pumps capped by adorable bows. When she spoke, I stopped staring and became attentive.

"Ladies, you have the honor, as well as the distinction of being the first women to be trained by the Army Airforces. Women pilots are badly needed, but because we're regarded as an experiment, you must prove your value and worth. You'll not have military status as of yet, and will be paid by the Civil Service Commission. You're entitled to access the PX for supplies. The factories are making thousands of new planes each month and they'll have to be moved to airbases around the country for our men to fly overseas in combat. You're not here to compete with or displace our male pilots, but to supplement them. I took 25 women pilots to England to ferry planes; I know it can be done. You have my faith. I have no fear, and I know you can do the job! I would now like to introduce to you General Henry H. Arnold."

We all applauded boldly. The general straightened the brim on his Army hat and made a low *"hem"* noise to stop the clapping. He was very tall and exuded power.

"Ladies, if you think you're hot pilots, I'd advise you to forget it. You're here to learn to fly the Army way, not like some private, fancy airport instructor might've taught you. Do not, at any time, tell anyone that you're flying for the Army and avoid all publicity until the WASPs are able to prove their worth. There are several ways you can wash out of here. One is by doing poorly in your class work; two, by failing too many flight tests; and three, by misbehaving and not obeying the Army rules. Most Americans find it unthinkable to put a woman in the cockpit of a military plane. Let's prove them wrong and help our men win this war. You are secret weapons waiting to be used. The Army allows six months to prove yourself, so ladies, let's see if you can learn to deliver our planes safely and on time!"

Director Cochran led the applause, as most of us were quite intimidated by the general's speech. "Girls, you may now go to your new living quarters. Enjoy the evening off and report for breakfast at the mess hall at 0600 hours sharp."

Director Cochran exited with the general.

We all walked off, and this was our last time *walking* to the low, stark, wood-framed barracks with bare cement floors that we were assigned to. Later on we were ordered to always march anywhere we went. There were six women in my bay and 12 of us had to share one puny little bathroom with only one large table for studying.

I flopped down on a skinny cot, exhausted from the new experiences of the day. On the bed next to me lay the tall, lanky girl who'd spoken to me earlier. She was smoking away and chattering between puffs.

"I'm Lana, from Bronx, New York. Where are you from?"

"Violet, from San Jose, California," I said. "Do you know anything about that cute cartoon figure on the entryway to the base?" I fluffed up the flat pillow, trying to get comfortable on the stiff, narrow cot.

"One of the officers said she's called Fifinella from Roald Dahl's book, *The Gremlins*. An artist named Walt Disney designed the cross-eyed, goggled gremlin with the spiral horns and eagle wings. She's our mascot." Lana wound her bouncy curls on her finger to tighten them.

"She's adorable," I said, glancing around the bare room. At the study table sat a very plain gal with an old-fashioned bob haircut. She sat there quite intently reading a bible.

"Hi, I'm May from Atlanta, Georgia," a girl in the next cot said to us in a sweet Southern drawl.

Next to May was a girl with wild, bushy blond hair.

"Where are you from?" I asked as I rolled onto my stomach, propping up my chin with my hands.

"Ask me no questions and I'll tell you no lies!" she said with enthusiasm.

Lana and I glanced at each other in wonderment, and both shot her odd looks.

"I'm Adele from Chicago." She laughed, moving her head, making her hair appear more unwieldy.

"We're from all over the States!" I exclaimed. Looking over at the bible-reading girl, I asked, "Where are you from?"

Startled, she glanced up and murmured, "La Porte, Indiana," then went back to her book.

"I Mei-lee," said a small girl with large, deep-brown, pollywog-shaped eyes.

Mei-lee went on to tell us that the Chinese Benevolent Society in Oregon had paid for her flight training, as well as training for many others. The society had financed the training ever since the Japanese invaded Manchuria in 1931.

We got to know each other well enough that first night to discover that flying was the one thing we all had in common, despite our different personalities and origins. I was very tired and didn't participate in the rest of the chitchat, drifting off to sleep with my clothes on. My dreams were made of worry as I stood facing a PT-19, feeling incapable of flying such a big airplane.

The sharp sound of reveille woke us with a start. Everyone quickly dressed. We threw on whatever we could pull from our suitcases, from heels to cowboy boots, since we hadn't been issued uniforms. I put on my worn-out coveralls. Every time the bathroom emptied out, several of us would dash in to wash up.

Lieutenant Borchardt was outside the barracks. She commanded us to line up and gave us a rudimentary lesson in marching to breakfast.

After we stood in the chow line, Lana, Adele, and I sat down at a long metal table.

I scooped a bite of gray-yellow eggs onto my fork, tasted them, and wrinkled my nose. I whispered to Lana, "Why does this not taste like eggs?"

"Because they're powdered and I suspect that mass of meat is brains, so watch out, because did you see that sign?" Lana pointed toward the front.

TAKE ALL YOU WANT
BUT EAT ALL YOU TAKE

"Thanks for the warning," I said, glad I had not taken any of the weird meat dish.

Adele looked at the sign. "Waste not, want not!"

Lana and I gave each other the eyebrow and went back to eating.

"Pass the critical butter," Adele shouted above all the clatter.

"What?" I asked confused, as well as annoyed.

She pointed at the sign in the corner of the mess hall that read: ***Butter is Critical.***

Lana and I chuckled, happy we didn't have to dig out our ration coupons here.

Before I knew it, the lieutenant presided over us. Between trying to eat the unusual breakfast and getting chummy with my new friends, I had lost track of time. We marched off to the administration building. Glancing around, I noticed all of us gals wore clothes that seemed to represent every state in America—my California farmer coveralls (with my good-luck pearl necklace hidden underneath), a three-piece tailored suit from Cleveland, and fancy cowboy boots from Oklahoma made up just a few of the outfits.

Director Cochran's stunning auburn hair cascaded down over one eye like Veronica Lake's. I couldn't keep my eyes off her. She was by far the most attractive lady I had ever seen in my life.

I snapped to attention when she said, "Ladies, here's your schedule—0600 hours is reveille, and 0700 begins ground school. You will have the following classes: physics, meteorology, maps, navigation, math, Morse code, military law, study of firearms, flight theory, instruments, and mechanics. At 1330 hours report to the flight line, where you'll begin practicing on our Primary Trainers, or PT-19s."

There was an excited "oooh" from the group, causing the director to glare at us. "I know you're all pilots, but you're here to learn to fly the Army way, and let me tell you, our planes are *not* little joyride airplanes like I'm sure most of you hobbyists are used to."

We all stood up straighter and kept our mouths shut.

"At 1900 hours is chow, then study time. Lights-out is at 2200 hours sharp. Every Saturday is white glove inspection." Director Cochran continued, "Before starting ground school, you will return to your barracks to find the only uniform the Army is able to provide. You now have exactly 30 minutes to try them on and report to the infirmary for your shots."

I glanced over at May. She had the same fearful expression on her face as I did on mine. The director's speech ended abruptly as she marched off, lightly flipping her hair.

Back at the barracks, we had a grand old time trying on the so-called uniforms.

"Which size do you want, shrimp? Large or large?" teased Lana as we tried on the surplus Army Airforce GI mechanic coveralls.

"Why, Violet, honey chile, y'all are swimmin' in them," May laughed, because she was almost as tall as Lana.

"You look a little better than I do," I said to May and Lana. "The size 44 Men's Large may put the crotch down to your thighs, but on me it goes to my knees! Look, the breast pocket is on my hip!" I laughed so hard it led to a coughing fit.

The olive drab, tent cloth, faded flight coveralls were all almost two sizes too big for each of us.

"Yippee, here are the belts, maybe they'll help." Adele flapped them around, hysterically laughing.

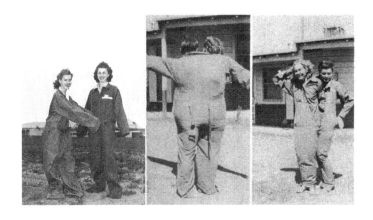

"Hey, Mei-lee, these are so big I bet two of us could fit in one," I shouted out amid the laughter.

Petite Mei-lee, always ready for a joke, got into my coveralls and we both paraded around as we bent over and wiggled our bottoms.

Lana, May, and Adele cinched up the huge, baggy, Harlem-like zoot suits, twirling and modeling while all the gals busted up laughing.

Rosemary was quiet, as usual. She tried hers on and just grinned at our antics while she hunted in her purse for safety pins.

I rolled up the arms and legs of my suit over and over, finally finding my hands and shoes. The suit flowed into a shapeless mass around my 5'1", 108-pound frame. The crotch was at my knees, and the shoulder seams hung over my elbows. Thank goodness there was a belt! Tears of hilarity rolled down my cheeks.

"I hate this stupid turban; it flattens out my curls," Lana complained. She was the only bay mate who had put curlers in her hair before going to bed the previous night. She had rolls and rolls of soft, dark-brown sausage curls and was by far the most attractive in the group.

Adele announced, "I actually like my turban."

Lana and I gave each other the eye. We were both probably thinking the same thought: *If I had your out-of-bounds hair, I'd like turbans, too!*

I looked at Adele closely. Her hair may have been unruly, but her butter-smooth face and likeable, twinkling eyes made up for it.

"I can't believe Director Cochran called these 'uniforms,'" Lana exclaimed, rolling her sleeves up more.

"At least we don't have to wear khaki underwear, like my cousin in the Army does," I added.

"Clothes don't make the man!" Adele quipped.

"It's obvious to me that, since we are classified as civilians, the Army sure enough won't waste a dime on us," May said in her contagious Southern drawl.

"Well, I don't even need a turban to keep my hair from flying around the cockpit 'cause I got my pigtails. If it wasn't for all the demerits, I'd be darned if I'd wear one of those," I exclaimed, pulling fondly at my hair.

A loud banging at the barracks door interrupted our fun.

"Time to go!" Mei-lee said.

Lieutenant Borchardt marched us off to the infirmary in our dreadful turbans and ridiculous flight suits, which contrasted sharply with her well-pressed Army uniform.

As we stood in the long line for the painful shots, Lana pushed up her sleeves and said, "I sure would like to know why we're getting all these shots when we'll never go overseas or near any combat zone."

I winced and cried out, "Ooh, these are going to hurt."

I marched behind Mei-lee to the flight line. On the black tarmac stood over 50 glimmering silver PT-19s. We were dazzled and quickly forgot about our sore arms from our shots. As we gasped with joy, Mr. Barnes, our instructor, gave us a sharp look.

Primary Trainer

"Ladies, this is the Fairchild Primary Trainer, or PT-19. It's a low-wing monoplane, with a 175-horsepower engine that cruises at 90 miles per hour. You'll have a total of three hours per week with an instructor in this two-seat tandem trainer. After you've had a total of 10 hours of instruction, there'll be a test on what we call a check ride. Your check ride won't be announced ahead of time—you must be prepared for it at a moment's notice. The instructor will grade you a Satisfactory or Unsatisfactory. If you get an unsatisfactory, you will have one more chance. If you get two U's, you may request a hearing before a board. If the board still doesn't grant a pass, then you'll wash right out of the program."

Adele whispered to me, "It would mean back to rearranging endless cans on a shelf in my parents' grocery store."

"How awful," I murmured back.

"I'm passing out a checklist for this type of ship and I expect you to memorize it by tomorrow," said Mr. Barnes. "That's all for now. Dismissed."

Mr. Barnes didn't march away, but instead walked off with a limp, which was probably why he wasn't overseas, I guessed.

The next morning, I awoke to Lana cursing at me. I couldn't believe I had actually slept past the wakeup bugle call.

"Damn it all to Hell, Violet, get your lazy ass up. It's time to march to chow, then calisthenics."

I looked at her bouncy curls, thinking that she had to get to bed late in order to roll her hair up every night.

"Lana, I never in my life have heard a girl, especially a Catholic, curse and smoke so much. Hold your horses and let me get on my exercise shoes."

"We are Yankee Doodle Pilots, born with a yearning to fly," sang out Adele as we marched out to the field. She sure looked better in a turban than exposing her messy do.

One of the inane Army rules said we weren't allowed

to talk while we marched everywhere, but were allowed to sing. I had been working on a marching song and tried it out on the way to ground school.

Once we wore scanties,

now we're in zoots

They are our issue GI flying suits

We look like a great big barrage

Oh, we've lost all our feminine gender

Our muscles are sore and tight

Our faces are wind burned and tender

We sure are a gruesome sight,

Ohhhh, we fly through the air in our little PTs

We spin and we stall with the greatest of ease

Our landings are rough

Our recoveries quick

Relax, little girl—pop that stick!

Everyone joined in. I felt a real sense of belonging, hearing my song being sung. I had to admit, all the constant marching did seem to boost our morale, and at the same time it gave us more energy.

"I'm a flying wreck, a riskin' my neck, and helluva pilot, too," Lana, Adele, Mei-lee, May, and I belted out as we marched to calisthenics. "Foxy" Ness, whose looks lived up to his name, barked out the calisthenics. Just having the pleasure of looking at him helped us get through the strenuous set of exercises. After calisthenics, Foxy demonstrated some Jiu-jitsu.

I leaned over and whispered to Adele, "This class is too hard; I'll never learn how to flip a 180-pound man over my shoulder."

"Your size doesn't help much, but I know what you mean. I wonder what this has to do with ferrying aircraft, anyway?" Adele said.

At the end of the class, Sergeant Ness announced, "Girls, you're all terrific pupils, but let me tell you, if some boy ever tries to bother you, forget all you learned in this class and just knee him in the groin. This is the oldest, fastest, and most proven method to really get back at a man, and don't ever forget it!"

We all roared with laughter, then clapped as the sergeant turned crimson red and went rapidly out of the classroom.

Marching off to another class around the wishing well, we sang, "Roll out the airplanes, we've got a big job to do," rewriting songs to fit our new lifestyle. This popular ditty we sang to the tune of "Roll Out the Barrel," a polka song.

There were training films on how to "ditch" an airplane in water during an emergency, as well as how to survive in a life raft in the Arctic. We even saw, by accident, a film on how to load ripe tomatoes into a railroad car.

The instructor used a small model plane to demonstrate a slow roll. It reminded me of my toy airplane and doll I used to play with as a kid.

We had to take all these courses to learn to fly the Army way. I lapped them up, remembering, in contrast, my dull English class in college. These classes were practical, and this made it easier for me to retain the knowledge.

Later that day, I anxiously waited to hear my name during mail call. It seemed everyone was getting a letter, even introverted Rosemary. At last, I heard "Violet" and quickly stepped forward, greedily tearing open a letter from Glenn.

Dear Violet:

Well, darling, congratulations are in order! My parents wrote and told me that you got into the WASPs. I am very proud of you.

I am with the Wildcat division and we are off to the Pacific. This is about all I can safely write about.

Please try not to worry if you don't hear from me while on this mission. I don't think it is possible to write, or know if it is even permitted.

I miss you sorely and hope you will be mine when this gosh darn war is over, then we can start a family of our own.

I love you with all my heart, Glenn

I couldn't believe my eyes. There was that marriage proposal again! I read it over and over, filled with the exhilaration of love.

After dinner, I jotted back a letter while listening to

the conversation in the bay.

"You know, Sweetwater is the rattlesnake capital of the world," Lana proclaimed, lighting up a Lucky with the one she'd just finished.

"I heard there is an annual rattlesnake round-up, when the town collects hundreds of them. Every type of poisonous snake in the USA is found right here in Texas," May drawled.

We all swapped stories, mostly about how strange the state of Texas was. All these gals and you'd think we would gab about boys, or even what we all had in common—flying. But then, nobody was from Texas and they wanted to talk about the weather or the weird creatures roaming about.

It was blasting hot and we dragged our cots outside to catch a breeze instead of sweating between the sheets. We had to tuck our blankets in snugly around us to protect ourselves from the dreaded snakes, black widow spiders, tarantulas, and scorpions crawling around. Mei-lee was voted the first one up to roust us all so we could scramble back inside to avoid getting a demerit before bugle call.

The following week, I squeezed in a moment to write a letter before lights-out. I propped myself up on the cot.

Dear Dad and Mother:

I am proud to say I passed the physical, as well as the interview with the renowned aviatrix Jacqueline

Cochran. Let me tell you, she is a forceful, determined, and powerful woman just like the newspapers say she is. Rumor has it that no one is ever able to say no to that lady, even the general!

The barracks are very primitive with no curtains or knick-knacks. If I wasn't so busy going to ground school and flying, I would be homesick.

I am lying on my Army cot, missing my own private room and being able to keep it as messy as I want. That was one good thing about having only brothers; I did get my own room!

There is no privacy here, as the bathrooms have no partitions and the shower area has only two spouts. You should see four or five of us scrambling to fit under the shower since we only have five to 10 minutes to wash up before going to chow. Each bay has six girls with cots, lockers, and one large table for studying. Twelve of us share a single bathroom!

Every Saturday is "white glove" inspection day. The blankets have to be tight enough for a quarter to bounce off of them! Sometimes I sleep on top of my blanket because I hardly have enough time in the morning to make my bed. The arrogant, chauvinistic lieutenants march into our bay with their white gloves, find a chocolate stain on the windowsill from a late-night snack, and then mark demerits in their little books. I wish I could say I don't care, but 70 demerits and you actually get washed right out of the program! One of my bunkmates, Adele, got a demerit just for leaving an apple in her locker.

There is endless, pointless marching to get to class or chow. We have to say "Yes sir" and "No sir" to all the instructors. All these Army rules and we are still just civilians. I just keep telling myself, if the Army can dish it out, then I can take it, just to get a chance to be in the sky.

Sweetwater, Texas, is a desolate desert. The wind blows all the time. I get dust in my teeth and have to even pick it out of my ears.

Mother, I sure miss and appreciate your cooking now. The mess hall food of powdered eggs and Spam is hard to swallow. Disgusting catfish is served every Friday and food poisoning is a common event around here.

I don't mean to complain, and I am grateful for all the classes I take, and especially the beautiful, beautiful ships they let us fly.

Kiss my little brothers for me,

Fondly, Violet

As I tucked the letter under my pillow, I felt dreadfully homesick. I searched under the neck of my nightgown for my pearl necklace, missing Mother, along with the comforts of home. I started to doubt my ability to meet all of the challenges of the WASPs. After tossing about on my narrow cot, I drifted off to sleep as my subconscious jumbled all my fears into one.

Chapter Nine: A Leave and the Link Trainer

At the end of the month, we were granted a free weekend leave. Adele called the Sweetwater carpool to arrange a ride into town.

"Are y'all comin'? Looks like y'all could use some excitement," May announced as she wiped off the cold cream that aided her smooth complexion.

"If you'd call the town of Sweetwater exciting," yawned Lana, who was from the big city of New York.

"I'm going. I heard there's a pool. We should bring our bathing suits," I said, rounding up a towel and suit.

I got up the nerve to ask May not to wear her Chanel No. 5 that day—I liked it, but I knew it would make me carsick in such a confined area. I was able to talk Rosemary into joining us. I was glad, because she looked lonely and I felt sorry for her.

The driver was a little old man with a sugary Texan accent. Mr. Shoemaker was happy to help the war effort and be of service to us good-looking young ladies. On the car ride, Lana got us all singing a song to the tune of "I've Been Working on the Railroad."

"I've been waiting on the flight line, just for a chance to fly,

I've been waiting on the flight line, for an hour in the sky

Can't you hear the props a-roaring, warming up on the line

Can't you hear the ships a-calling, come Fifinella, fly."

Lana was flapping her arms while singing, when all of a sudden one of the retreads went flat. Mr. Shoemaker pulled off the edge of the narrow, two-lane road. In doing so, the right wheels of the car sank into the soft shoulder. It was now too low to slip the jack under. Our determined driver then tried to push the car, but without success.

"The poor, sweet man. I hope he can get us out," said May, a worry wrinkle forming between her eyebrows.

"We can help you, sir," I exclaimed with my usual sunny attitude.

"Let us help," Adele said. "Many hands make light work!"

Lana and I rolled our eyes.

Mr. Shoemaker, being a proper gentleman, wiped the sweat off his brow. "Now, ladies, don't y'all fret. I can take care of this little situation." He continued to rock the automobile with his shoulder, but with little reward.

We talked him into letting us take a spot along the back bumper and sides of the automobile.

Bossy Lana shouted, "On the count of three, lift. ONE, TWO, THREE!"

We hoisted the car into the air. Mr. Shoemaker shoved

the jack into place as his eyes bugged out from all the straining. He shook his head, saying over and over, "My, my, my."

Our efforts made it possible for him to change the tire, and soon we were on our way. Calisthenics barked out by Sergeant Ness proved to have given us strength we didn't even know we had.

At last, we reached the town of Sweetwater. We thanked Mr. Shoemaker, got out of the car, and looked around. The town seemed to be only one block long with just a few buildings. A mother with two children attached to her looked us up and down, then purposely crossed to the other side of the street, even after Lana tried a cheerful hello. An older gentleman in a gray felt hat strolled by, giving us a suspicious look.

"Hey chums, let's duck into the movies to escape the staring from the townsfolk," Adele said, pointing to a small theater down the street.

"Good idea. I'm getting tired of them glaring at our baggy zoot suits," Lana said, cinching her belt and arranging her curls.

Once we were sitting in the cool dark, I quietly said to May, "Bela Lugosi gives me the heebie jeebies."

May whispered back, "Vampires are supposed to do that, honey."

After the movie we stopped at the Blue Bonnet Café. Lana, May, Adele and I ordered Coca-Colas and Rosemary ordered a cup of hot water. We all gave her an odd look as she shyly pulled a tea bag from her pocket.

Adele leaned into my ear. "Maybe her elevator doesn't go all the way to the top."

I chuckled to keep Adele quiet, hoping she wouldn't say anything further and embarrass us.

It was extremely humid out, and we were glad we had brought our bathing suits, except for Rosemary, who said she had "forgotten" hers. Swimming in the town pool proved to be a terrific idea. The locals warmed up to us more, especially after I helped a little girl practice her floating. She was adorable, with blond pigtails that matched mine, except a shorter version.

"Why, thanks, young lady, for teaching my Kathleen to float. I've been trying all summer," the little girl's mother said, checking the zipper in the back of her daughter's swimsuit.

"I love kids," I answered. I missed my little brothers.

"My name's Mrs. Sampson," she smiled.

"Glad to meet you. I'm Violet Willey. These are my friends, Lana Walton, May Whitmore, Adele Watts and Rosemary Wright. We're in training at Avenger…" I left the sentence hanging, remembering that we were not allowed to talk about being pilots.

Adele leaned into me and whispered, "Loose lips sink ships."

I blushed as Mrs. Sampson asked, "Why do y'all have last names starting with W?"

"We're all in the same barracks, which are alphabetized, so we're part of the W group," said Adele, undoing the strap on her bathing cap.

"The whole town's been talking about girls flying airplanes! You certainly don't seem dangerous. I'd love to invite y'all to dinner," said Mrs. Sampson.

We all were visibly relieved that the secret was out.

Brash Lana spoke up first, speaking for all of us. "That'll be swell."

"No clock is more regular than the belly," Adele added, making my cheeks turn pink.

The dinner at the Sampson family farm was a delicious, home-cooked meal.

"Thanks, Mrs. Sampson, your fried chicken is heavenly," Adele beamed.

"And the rhubarb pie," I added.

"Everything tastes wonderful, but it makes me homesick," Rosemary said sadly.

"Thank you kindly, ma'am," May said.

"You're more than welcome, girls. I'm happy to get to know you all. Some of the townspeople have taken bets on how many airplanes you gals would manage to crash. Why, Mrs. Turner won't even let her children out in the yard to play when she hears one go by! I feel more confident about your intelligence after sharing a meal with all of you. I'll make sure I get the good word out to my neighbors that you're all not such a bad lot."

We left on the last bus with our bellies full. I was pleased that we were able to smooth the gap between the WASPs and the townspeople.

We all had to have 19 hours of practice in the link trainer. This was a little box that had stubby little wings and a tail. It simulated flying under any conditions, which allowed us to safely practice before going up in a real airplane. The link trainer was painted canary yellow. Was this a cruel joke for us trainees to pretend it was a Piper Cub?

I lay awake going over all the instruments we'd been learning. I knew that by mastering the link trainer, I could fly in any weather and even at night. I was just about to drift off, saying to myself over and over, "Trust in the instruments, trust in the instruments," when I heard Rosemary next to me mumbling, "Unlock controls, push rudder, thrust stick." I wasn't the only one keyed up and obsessed about the next day's test in the trainer.

The next day in the classroom, I whispered to Lana, "I just want to fly. I'm getting sick of this toy airplane that never lifts off the ground!" I bit my pencil.

"I'm with you on that one," Adele whined. "Instrument flying is an unnatural act, probably punishable by God. It's a claustrophobic torture chamber!"

"God Almighty, you two, stop your bellyaching," Lana said. "We've had one month to learn over 50 instruments on the link trainer. If we trust in the instruments, we can ferry the biggies through the wild blue yonder, blindfolded!" Lana illustrated her exasperation by shuffling her notes together roughly.

The civilian instructor, Red Timberton, shouted, "Violet, yer up!"

I had seen red hair before, but not flaming red, as his was—so bright it looked like it was on fire. I tried not to gape at him.

"Yes, sir," I said nervously as I walked to the front of the classroom, where I accidentally bumped into one of the desks before getting into the flight simulator.

Instructor Timberton sat at a large map table that had a repeated display of the main flight instruments. The wings and tail section of the trainer had control surfaces that actually moved in response to the pilot's movement of the rudder and stick.

I put on the earphones. The black hooded canvas covering the cockpit was over my head and I proceeded to sweat in the hot box, waiting for instructions. Using only the instruments in the dark little box, I manipulated the controls, causing the box to rotate and pitch on its pivot. "Overrule the brain and trust in the instruments," I mumbled to myself. Instructor Timberton controlled the turbulence, or wind force in any direction, and the fuel gauge.

"Flaps!" Red yelled.

I frantically groped for the handle. I found the lever and pulled it down.

"Landing gear."

Blindly, I fumbled until I found the right knob. Half the time I thought I was turning right when I was turning left, but I repeated "trust in the instruments" to myself, which soothed me.

I knew the test was over when the instructor shouted, "Congratulations, Violet, you passed. Lana, yer up!"

I had passed the link trainer test, mastering being "under the hood," which made me proficient in locating any item in the cockpit without having to visually hunt for it. Relieved it was over, I wiped the sweat off my forehead and gave Lana a thumbs-up. She whispered to me, "Stick around, I need you to help me with something."

When her test was finished, Lana hopped out of the little yellow box.

Timberton announced, "Satisfactory, Miss Walton."

"Congratulations, Lana. Now, what did you want me to help you with?" I asked.

"I can't draw for beans. Come with me to make a wreath," Lana said, heading to the far right wall in the link trainer classroom.

Oh, no, I thought as I followed her toward the back of the room. I had seen the small funeral wreaths spread all over the wall since the class had started a month ago. I was barely 20 years old and had yet to know anyone killed in the war. It frightened me to hear how many of my young classmates had experienced this.

"Right here, Vi, draw me a wreath for Rosemary." Lana pointed on the wall.

"Did she crash?" I asked, fingering the dents on my worn pencil.

"She sure did! I hope she passes the next time, then she can keep up with us."

I drew the small funeral wreath while Lana added "Rosemary" in the middle.

"She'll laugh her head off when she sees this tomorrow," Lana said, chuckling.

I shook my head, thinking that I had never seen

Rosemary laugh. I remained quiet because I didn't like how all the gals joked about death. Adele especially liked singing the nasty, morbid song, "Blood in the Cockpit" when we marched to link training class.

That night, a few of us wore our only pair of coveralls in the shower and soaped them up. I laid mine out at the bottom of my bed to dry, stretched out in my wet underwear, and opened a card from Mother.

Dearest Violet:

Your father and I were happy to hear from you and that you are safe. Happy Birthday! The war is in full power now and I suppose you are really needed. We have plenty of ration coupons because we live on a farm, unlike the city people, who never seem to have enough.

I am glad the boys are too young to join up, even though your father would be proud to send them. Then our family could do its part to win the war.

I ran into Mrs. Conney the other day. She also hasn't heard from Glenn. Will keep you posted.

I hope you don't need any money. Since the war, we've been on a very tight budget. Your father, as usual, is very proud of you. Enclosed is a newspaper article about the WASPs. Please be careful and take care,

Love, Mother

P.S. I hope you are taking care of the pearl necklace I gave you.

SAN JOSE MERCURY TRIBUNE

Jacqueline Cochran is an amazing woman who has set more speed, distance, and altitude records than any other pilot, male or female. She has successfully established the Women Airforce Service Pilots. The WASPs help ferry airplanes from the factories to the Army bases. She is proving to the Army that girls can fly anything it builds. So far, women pilots' failure rate is the same as male cadets. The girls tend to study more diligently and are faster on instruments than the boys.

The trainees are subject to Army discipline and regulation, but remain under civilian status. Upon graduation, the girls will be competent to fly any size Army air trainer and will have the groundwork for flying fast combat planes.

Commanding General Henry H. Arnold said he was skeptical about putting young girls into the cockpits of planes, but Britain and Russia have already been successful in doing this. There is a severe shortage of male pilots at home. The WASPs are badly needed, and he supports Director Cochran 100 percent in the mass training of girl pilots.

I got out a pen and paper and wrote a letter back to my parents.

Dear Mother and Dad:
Thank you for the birthday card. Much to my surprise, the cooks made me a cake and all the gals sang Happy Birthday to me during chow!

It is another sweltering, roasting, 100-degree Texas night. The locals tell us it stays 100 degrees from April to September. I sure miss the even climate of San Jose.

Even though we were exhausted from ground school, my bay mates and I had an ice water fight, then fell off to sleep on our drenched sheets. I haven't laughed that hard in all my life. I think I found the sisters I never had! I feel joyful to be surrounded by all these hardworking, dedicated gals.

Being here is both wonderful and troublesome, as I'm constantly nervous about washing out. Well, must close now to get some shut-eye.

Love, Violet

P.S. Don't worry about me; I do get some money for this Civil Service work and go to the PX to get inexpensive supplies. Thank you again for Grandma's string of pearls, I always wear them up in the sky as a good-luck charm.

I glanced across the large study table at Rosemary reading her bible. She always fit in her religion despite our tight schedule. Sometimes I saw her reading it under her covers using a flashlight after lights-out. Maybe that was why she failed the link trainer test, because she didn't get enough sleep. I decided I would add her to my nightly prayers. I was grateful I had studied enough to pass the instrument test in the link trainer. Next week, I was scheduled to fly under a hood in a real plane in the sky. Just the thought left me feeling terrified.

Chapter Ten: The Check Ride

The following week I got to fly in a brand new BT-13, fully equipped for instrument flying. The instructor rode in the front seat, ready to take the controls in case I made a mistake. A black hood was pulled over the student's cockpit, so all I could see were the instruments: the clock, airspeed indicator, altimeter, and compass. I had to fly a precise four-leg pattern.

Sergeant Solesky spoke into the radio. "Now, climb to 500 feet on the first leg, make a turn of exactly 360 degrees, fly level on the second leg, make a turn of 270 degrees and descend 500 feet on the third leg."

I was sweating during the whole flight since there were 50 planes in our local airspace at any given time, and I couldn't see any of them.

After we landed, the sergeant jumped out and said, "You're doing good, Violet; I had my doubts at first when I saw your size, but you've proved me wrong!"

"Thanks, sir," I said with a pleased grin, clutching my height-adding cushion. While marching back to the barracks, I felt quite stirred up, thinking of how many airplanes I would eventually learn to fly now that I'd passed my instrument test.

When I opened the door to our barracks, I saw Lana squeezing her fingers. "Holy mother of God," she yelled. "Looks like Rosemary didn't make it!"

"You mean she's...gone?" I looked over at Rosemary's cot, which was completely bare. "I wish we could've said goodbye." My bottom lip trembled.

May sank down on her bunk. "She sure tried hard enough, but she flunked her second instrument test today."

"From what I could tell, she was an excellent pilot, but when she went under the hood in that small box she got claustrophobic." Lana nonchalantly lit a Lucky Strike, looked into her pocket mirror, and reshaped her eyebrows with a moistened finger.

I solemnly walked into the bathroom, crying quietly to myself, mostly with relief at having passed my check ride, but also with great sorrow for my bay mate's abrupt departure.

May came in and found me bawling in the corner. She put her arm around me and whispered, "There, there, honey, just let it all out." I breathed in her Chanel No. 5, feeling comforted.

Lying on my cot, I tried to put the sadness of Rosemary's washing out behind me by saying a little prayer. "Lord, protect and surround me. Fifinella, fly closely on my shoulder." To get my mind off Rosemary's absence, I tried going over all the maneuvers in my mind in case I had another check ride tomorrow. Tossing and turning, I knew I was getting a bad case of "check-itis."

The next morning, after a fitful sleep, I marched out to the flight line carrying my usual two cushions so I could see out the window of the plane. I brought along the custom blocks that I had made in town to tie onto my oxfords so my feet could reach the pedals. My heavy parachute pack banged against the back of my knees.

Lieutenant Hockett gave me a sneer that made me feel even more insecure. Looking at all six feet of him, with his mean, narrow gray eyes, I optimistically produced my biggest smile.

All he did was shake his head while muttering to himself, "Aviation is a man's field. Why's this puny kid trying to fly a plane?" Then he said to me, "All you dames look alike with no figures in those men's coveralls."

I took in a breath of fresh air to calm myself down, knowing that he certainly did not expect me to answer such a rude comment. He was so conceited as he swaggered toward the plane. I followed behind him.

With the brakes set and the stick pulled back, he swung the propeller. As it came to life, he scrambled into the front seat. We bumped over the rough ground, wings dipping from side to side, as we taxied out for takeoff.

Once up in the crowded air, a careless plane came directly at us. Lieutenant Hockett jerked the controls away from my hands and jammed the throttle wide open to pull above the oncoming plane. It passed so close under us that the celluloid windows rattled violently. When I looked down to see what kind of airplane it was, he shot me a nasty look.

Lieutenant Hockett screamed at me through the Gosport tube, "God damn it, watch your direction!"

I choked back the tears, thinking, *I'm not a quitter; I'll give it all I've got.* I knew I dared not let my emotions get away from me. Men were dying every day in battles for the war. I had to swallow my failure and try again. After all, Mother always said, "practice makes perfect," even though she was only talking about pies. I knew all of us WASPs had to do better than the men, or be scorned.

Unfortunately, Hockett was the typical male pilot with the attitude that I had often heard about. I thought about Rosemary, and didn't want to end up with the same fate.

The lieutenant barked orders, grabbed the stick from

me, and knocked it back and forth against my knees. He swore and flew into a rage again. "Damn it, watch your airspeed!"

With all his abusive cursing, I had trouble concentrating. I maneuvered toward the right.

"Seatbelt!" he shouted in my headphones.

In shock, I felt myself slip out of the plane. Instinctively, I pulled my parachute cord, remembering from class that it must be done at a high altitude in order to land safely. Counting to a rapid 10, the chute fluttered open and I floated down toward a field. After the initial shock of falling out of the plane, all I could think was—*I DID have my seatbelt on. I did!*

I waited in the field for Lieutenant Hockett to pick me up. Then I noticed the seatbelt a few feet away from me, lying in the grass.

I managed to wipe away my tears as the lieutenant arrived.

"Christ, the mechanics never secured the belt to the seat. Get back in!" he grumbled.

I got back into the cockpit. Even though there was no seatbelt, I still had the single-minded dedication to make it through the check ride and not wash out.

Toward the end of our flight, Hockett took over, even though I should have been the one learning. My eyes filled with tears, but I tried not to show any emotion.

Finally, we landed. One of the instructors shouted, "Where've you two been?"

The lieutenant jumped out and threw off his parachute, yelling in front of everyone, "Goddamn dame doesn't know what she's doing!"

I got out, feeling a hot flush on my cheeks. There was an entire male audience before me.

Hearing nasty snickering, one of the male pilots announced to his buddies, "Broads shouldn't be flying!"

Then they all burst into laughter, as one of the mechanics said, "No wonder she couldn't land it. Look at the size of her! I bet her dainty little feet can't even reach the pedals!"

The humiliation bothered me, even though I had done nothing wrong. I stomped off toward the hangar just as a male student landed his plane, bouncing several times. The same man said, "Looks like old Hal is having a bad morning!"

I shook my head. I thought the airplane didn't care whether the pilot was a male or female. It boiled down to who could handle the dang thing. A fast airplane demanded a skilled person, not a particular sex.

That night in the shower I noticed my legs were black and blue.

"How'd your check ride go, Violet sugar?" May asked, folding her clothes into her locker.

"Pretty bad," I said, grinding my teeth.

"Why, honey? Who was your check pilot?"

"Lieutenant Hockett," I said, rubbing the bruises on my legs.

"Land sakes, no wonder; he hates all of us WASPs. You better request someone else on your second try so you don't wash out," May said, concerned.

I learned that in the Army, standards were high, and errors in judgment were not tolerated. Sure, we were told that if we had a personality clash with the instructor we could request a change, but we all believed it would just aid in getting us washed out. Lana would always say, "If I flunk it means returning home to be chained to a typewriter every day." All of us shared the obsession—the passion—to fly. No obstacle could get in the way of satisfying this strong desire.

Wearily flopping on my cot, I wrote a letter to Glenn. I tried to keep it as positive as possible, since I knew his challenges in the Pacific were far greater than mine.

Dearest Glenn:

I miss you! I think of you often, especially when I practice many of the aerobatics you taught me in these beautiful PT-19s. I can't wait to pass my final check ride to go on to the advanced trainers. I imagine you get to fly some beauties, also. I fly in a very crowded airspace with many pilots training at the same time. Why, more than 400 trainees have arrived since I came. The other half of the day, I am in ground school. You would be very proud to see me take apart an entire airplane engine and then correctly put it back together again!

Good luck on your mission. I hope it will not be too dangerous. I know you will do your best for our country, but be careful. And yes, I would love to settle down and have children with you!

I miss you with all my heart,

Violet

It was Saturday again, which meant the dreaded white glove inspection. This was how we were introduced abruptly to the Army way. We went with a fury, hitting two-inch cockroaches in our barracks with a phone book. The smartly uniformed lieutenants entered the bay with constant scowls on their faces. Anxiously, we all stood at attention in our leather oxfords, which were shined to perfection.

Lana whispered to me, "Where does the Army find such mean officers?"

I wondered, too, since we never saw these men around the base. Averting my eyes from Lana, I hoped the lieutenants hadn't seen her talking to me.

The two officers went along with their white gloves to see if there was any dust, or even water in the sink. We were all flustered, knowing we could actually get washed out from accumulating too many gigs. Next, they stood on chairs, white-gloving the beams of the ceiling.

May murmured to Adele, "All these Army rules and we aren't really even in the Army!"

They started marking demerits in their little books while sneering and peeping around. The lieutenants found a chocolate bar wrapper in one of the beds, even soap scraps on the side of the shower. We never really got what "spotless" meant, though we were not sloppy types. Just then I saw something terrible. Adele had left her girdle soaking in suds in a basin. The officers found socks hanging over the shower rod and crackers with cheese under Mei-lee's bed. The tension in the room was so high you could cut it with a knife. Only 70 demerits could wash us right out.

The first lieutenant held out his book as the other officer looked on, saying, "Willey, one demerit; Walton, two."

After listing every one of us, the thin, taller one said smugly, "Better luck next time, ladies!"

The self-righteous officers departed. We moved our cots outside.

"I passed my first solo flight yesterday," Lana told everyone as we tucked in our sheets, still afraid of all the many Texas critters of the night, like the black widow spiders, scorpions, and snakes.

"Congratulations," I said, glancing at her as she rolled her curls.

"It would've been more rewarding, except that when I looked out over my left wing there was a seven-foot-long rattler slowly inching its way up toward the cockpit. It was the biggest, fattest, longest, scariest snake I ever saw in my life! I pushed the throttle to go faster and the wind caught the snake and it whipped off, thank God!" Lana's hands flew all over the place as she told the story.

"Ooh, I hate snakes!" Mei-lee said, shuddering a little. "I get shoes with straps next time we go to town."

Like most of the other gals around her, solo piloting a BT-13 was never as frightening to Lana as the Sweetwater snakes. After hearing Lana's story, we all resolved to check our cockpits before getting in.

"Did y'all get thrown in the wishing well?" asked May, folding down the lace on her silky nightgown.

"You bet your sweet ass I did," Lana proudly swore. "That's the best reward for a solo, especially on these scorching Texas days."

"I wish I'd get called to do my solo soon," I announced.

"I hope I'm around to throw you in!" said Lana, chuckling. She pushed a bobby pin into one of her curlers.

As I lay on my back under the bright, star-studded night, the moon lit up my newsletter.

FIFINELLA GAZETTE

Lieutenant Colonel Curry had a picture of Fifi painted on a P-40.

Saturday night's bonfire celebrated the tossing-in of all the dreaded turbans. The Army declared an end to wearing them.

Today's flying tips: Ladies, check your cockpits before getting in; beware of those Texas rattlers.

One out of three WASPs seems to wash out. Don't despair; this is the same record for the male cadets. The Army has found that boys compete more, while girls will help each other out. Hurray for our team!

Remember gals, the future of the Army Airforces rests on your shoulders. Salute to Fifinella, she's

the one keeping sand out of our gas tanks, our
engines running smooth, and is responsible for our
good takeoffs as well as safe landings.

KEEP 'EM FLYING, FIFINELLA!

Just in case I was called for a solo flight test the next
day, I went up to the huge, 20-foot circular stone wishing
well to throw in my lucky, shiny penny. Kissing it first, I
said my usual prayer. "Lord, protect and surround me
with Your love." As I marched off, I added, "Fifinella,
guide me and stay closely on my shoulder, be my
guardian angel."

I met Instructor Bucker at the flight line the next day.
He said with a grin, "All right, Violet, yer up for solo.
Those are quite the overalls. I can't even see your figure in
them." He gave me the onceover.

"I'm ready," I said, feeling uncomfortable as he
continued to stare. I was getting pretty tired of the
officers' comments on our so-called uniforms. I looked
away, adjusting my bulky parachute pack.

"I want you to fly two hours from Avenger Field, land,
and then return," he said, slipping his pen onto his
clipboard.

"Yes, sir," I said, and climbed onto the wing to the
cockpit with my blocks and cushions. In the pocket of my
mechanic's suit I felt around for a compass and watch. My
map was attached to my knee with a rubber band—then it
wouldn't fly out the open cockpit like it did once before.

121

The other knee held a notepad and pencil. On the leg of my pants, I had placed a wide strip of white adhesive tape to jot down the takeoff and landing time in big pencil numbers. I was well prepared to pass my solo. I had calculated the speed, altitude, taken into account the wind direction, and checked the weather report for the conditions of the day. For good luck, I had on my string of pearls.

Up I went in the PT-19. It was glorious, fast, strong, and powerful. I looked at my map each time I passed a checkpoint, then glanced at my watch to make sure I was passing each one on time. My first problem was that I couldn't find the train tracks that were clearly marked on my map. *Relax, relax,* I told myself, as I knew tension and anxiety led to mistakes. As soon as I spotted a familiar town, the marvelous feeling of flying drifted around me. I filled my lungs with air, breathing deeply while enjoying the wispy cirrus clouds high above. I enjoyed watching the shadow of my miniature twin PT-19 always at my side. If only I could find the railroad tracks, then I could follow them to the next town to be really sure of where I was. Calming myself, I hummed a little ditty May had made up to the tune of "Deep in the Heart of Texas":

We damn near freeze

In these open PTs

Deep in the heart of Texas

If you don't lock the latch,

You'll fall out of the hatch

Deep in the heart of Texas!

The Texas sky was turning an ominous gray and a light rain began to fall. I would be soaked before the flight was over. I wiped the drops off my goggles. The weather report was wrong, and I certainly was fooled by how nice it had been at the beginning of the flight. I might have had the hours, but was apprehensive because I had only flown in good weather. Oh, my little Fifinella, where were you?

Chapter Eleven: The Solo and Lana's Escapade

It was easy to get lost without mountain peaks or ranges to follow like those in California. Flying across the Midwest was harder to navigate because the landscape was very flat and never-ending. The map didn't have enough landmarks, just squiggly contour lines for hills. I buzzed the railway station to read the name of the town, located it on the map, and then was able to draw a new course to my destination.

Once the weather cleared, I was overjoyed to know where I was. I practiced my loops, chandelles, and pylong eights. I just loved how handy some of the aerobatics could be to help me change direction more quickly. Shooting up into the air, I made a beautiful loop. I was concentrating so hard trying to master the exact precision of the move that when I was done with my aerobatics, I had lost my markers back to home base. I flew around in each direction looking for a familiar landmark without success. I felt foolish that I had wasted so much time. I now only had two hours of fuel left in my tank.

Just as panic began to set in, Lana flew reassuringly into view. She saved me. I followed her on a steady westward course. I gave her the thumbs-up for a thank you.

Then, I remembered what my instructor had told me in college. "Flying is the second greatest thrill known to man; landing is the first!" I was definitely looking forward to landing soon.

All of a sudden I was starving. I reached down into my knee pocket and pulled out a squishy peanut butter and jelly sandwich and wolfed it down.

At last, the checkpoints were exactly like the map. I made it back safely and on time. Since there was no radio on this model plane, I had to land when the green signal light pointed toward me.

"Congratulations, Miss Willey," Instructor Bucker said as he thrust out his hand. "You've just passed your solo."

"Thanks, Mr. Bucker." I pumped his hand with enthusiasm.

Lana, May, Adele, and Mei-lee greeted me with a "Hip hip hooray!" We all marched off to the wishing well, where they grabbed my arms and legs. They threw me in, my braids flying behind me. I retrieved a lucky penny, feeling wonderfully satisfied with my latest accomplishment. I was soaking wet, but it felt marvelous in the humid, sticky heat.

On my day off, I decided to catch up on my letter writing.

Dear Cuz:

How has Army life in South Carolina been treating you?

I have some free time and I am writing to you in my bathing suit. I am stretched out on my towel over the dirt, with my upside-down wooden chair to lay my head on to keep my braids out of the dust!

I hope you can get a pass to make it to my graduation ceremony in a few months.

Write me back,

Love, Cuz Violet

I pulled my short towel down to cover my feet better and read the base newsletter.

THE FIFINELLA GAZETTE

COCHRAN'S CONVENT:

Over 40 male flyers from other bases started making forced landings here with various mysterious complaints about engines running rough. Director Cochran got wind of this and has now closed off the entire base to other planes, except for "real" emergencies. As we all know, dating is strictly forbidden; now it is next to impossible!

In the first issue of the *Gazette*, the director wrote a story about a sprite that pulled pranks on her. Walt Disney has immortalized Fifi, and now we have someone to blame for all our troubles: the fog, missing runways, maps flying out of the cockpit, and even sputtering engines!

Buy a leather patch of "Fifi" at the PX to sew on your "uniform."

The locust infestation this year at the base has been terrible. At first we wondered whether the large, black cloud would bring in a storm. After the second day we picked grasshoppers out of our hair. Then one of the gals skidded a plane on the flight line because of them.

The Avenger Field rite of passage is being thrown in the wishing well after soloing. See photo below of Violet Willey being thrown in with her pigtails flying out behind her!

Passing the solo and being thrown in the wishing well. Jacqueline Cochran on far right.

127

Lana Walton's new marching song (to the tune of "Home on the Range"):

Oh, I'm far from home

Where the wild Texans roam,

Where the snakes and tarantula play,

Where seldom is heard

An encouraging word

And we never have time to make hay.

A WASP trainee I am—

Sunburned, dusty and dry.

There's no time to play.

They work us all day.

Volunteers are we and never know why!

If I graduate

I'll get out of this state

And never see Texas no more—

We'll ferry their planes

Through the winds and the rains

And help all our boys win the war.

KEEP 'EM FLYING, FIFINELLA!

I turned over the *Gazette* flyer and wrote a letter to my parents on the back, knowing how much Dad would love reading it.

Dear Dad and Mother:

It's like a revolving door around here. I've been feeling blue; three more girls washed out this month and then two actually quit the WASPs.

A bay mate in Barracks S slit her wrists right before her solo and got discharged for emotional instability. Our bay gets smaller, and then two new recruits arrive. I am having trouble being friendly to them, protecting myself from feeling hurt, in case they wash out. I'm glad I inherited your tenacity and willpower, Dad.

We are all licensed pilots, but the military aspect of the WASPs is a whole different can of worms. From cleaning our bay, to marching, and having to eat everything on our plate, I ask you—what does this have to do with flying?

Mother, I received your package of homemade peanut butter cookies. They were delicious and made me a little homesick.

Now for the good news. You can be very proud parents. I passed link trainer and went on to pass my solo. Graduation, here I come!

Have you heard from Glenn's mother? I have written him three letters and still no response.

All my Love, Violet

The next night, Lana wanted to sneak out. She was completely smitten with her instructor, Gus. I did think he was extremely attractive with his strawberry-specked blond hair. I loved looking at his big, broad shoulders, and he was the tallest man I had ever laid my eyes on—a good match for lanky Lana. I still felt this scheme of Lana's was not worth the risk, especially after watching so many gals wash out. We were close to graduating, and I decided to try to talk her out of it.

I watched Lana fussing in the mirror. First, she undid her pin curls. Next, she pulled out the Goody aluminum end curlers, and then removed the bobby pins from the clockwise row onto the counterclockwise row of finger waves. Just watching her deal with her fussy hair was exhausting to me as I twisted my simple pigtails.

"What's up?" Lana questioned as I intently watched her brush her long rolls of glamorous waves.

"I have to admit, you do manage to pull off the Hollywood look."

"Really? Who do you think I look like?" She brushed her gorgeous hair over and over.

"Actually, like Lana Turner," I said, pushing one of her rollers around on her cot.

Lana gave me a huge smile as she put on her bright-red lipstick. Smoothing her large lips together, she blotted them on a piece of toilet paper, and then made a kissing noise at me. I let out a friendly chuckle as she opened a jar of Cylax Stockingless Cream.

She smeared it up and down each leg, sighing, "I miss my silk stockings. Too bad parachutes need to be produced instead. Here, draw my seams." She handed me an eyebrow pencil. "You know, I'm the oldest of four sisters and I'm happy to have my own lipstick and rollers without one of them stealing them from me."

"I never had problems like that, I only have brothers." I carefully made a straight line down her long legs.

Lana looked behind herself, then asked, "How are they?"

"I made pretty good lines and it does look like you're wearing stockings."

"Humm, I seem to be missing an important accessory," Lana said, gazing into the locker mirror.

"What's that?" I wondered.

"Could I borrow your pearl necklace?" Lana's casual tone told me she was used to borrowing things. I certainly wasn't.

"They're very valuable to me." I held my pearls firmly around my neck.

"Please, Violet, I promise I'll cherish them. Besides, they'll surely bring me good luck as they always do for you." She fluttered her long, mascara-coated lashes.

"Lana, I must be honest with you. I'm uncomfortable about you sneaking out to see Gus. I don't think I could bear graduating without you." I looked away from her glamour get-up, nervously buttoning and unbuttoning my coveralls.

She squeezed my hand. "I'm very flattered you care

about me that much, but don't worry. I'll make it back for bed check."

I squeezed her hand back, took off my necklace, stretched up on my toes, and put it around her neck.

"Oooo, that's the perfect final touch, thanks. I really want Gus to give me the WOW look," Lana said, waving her startling red-polished nails while twirling a pearl on the necklace. "Now for the hard part. Help me get over the fence."

We walked into the dark, outside the barracks toward the eight-foot-high fence.

"Christ Almighty, Violet, keep pushing!"

"You're much bigger than me; I'm pushing as hard as I can."

Lana stretched as high as she could to get to the top of the fence. "You little pipsqueak, just go find a footstool!"

I ran back to the barracks, grabbed a stool, and beat it back to the fence. I knew Lana had very little time for a date, and barely enough to make it back for the 12:00 bed check.

Sleep could not find me that night as Mr. Worry took over. I turned back and forth, getting up every half hour to look at the clock on the study table. "God save us," I murmured, surprising myself as Mother's most dreaded expression escaped from my mouth. At 11:45, I quickly went through Lana's clothes and made her bed up like a body, hoping and praying the scam would work. I didn't think I could cope with being here if Lana washed out. We had become very close over the past six months.

Just like clockwork, some mysterious lieutenant marched in at midnight, looking from bed to bed, shining a flashlight on each one. I exhaled suddenly, not even realizing I had been holding my breath during the entire inspection. I quickly coughed to cover up my noise. The lieutenant shined the light toward me and I mumbled, "Excuse me." The officer went to the door and finally left.

With her beau's help, Lana slipped back in at 1:00 a.m., having thoroughly enjoyed her romantic rendezvous.

Though I was half asleep, I managed to scold her. "Was your little adventure really worth almost getting washed out?"

"Yes, Vi, he's a hunk of a heartbreak! Thank Fifinella I didn't get caught, and I'm grateful to you for that extraordinary bed trick!"

"You're welcome. Better get some shut-eye. There's only five hours till reveille." A rhythmic throbbing spread in my head, preventing the needed sleep from returning. How was I ever going to fly the next day with so little rest?

I kept blinking my eyes and refocusing them in the PT-19 the following morning.

"Sir, this PT-19 is handling mighty rough." I raised my voice while speaking into the Gosport.

"I was thinking the same thing," Sergeant Brown said as he checked over the instruments once again. Just as he looked up, the fuel tank abruptly caught on fire.

"Oh my God, you better bail out, Violet. I'll land her over in the field," I heard him shout in my earphones.

My body shook as I quickly jumped out of the plane, pulling the ripcord on my chute. Floating down, I couldn't believe my bad luck. There I was, using a parachute for the second time, when not one of my bay mates had even done so once. I almost enjoyed the free-fall, until my imagination let loose and I worried about landing on sagebrush, cactus—or worse, a pile of rattlesnakes. My ankle turned when I fell, but I quickly straightened it out in order not to break it. Descending in the middle of a desolate pasture, all I could think about was Texas rattlers. I spread out the parachute, sat in the middle of it, and waited to be rescued. The hot Texas sun was blistering. Suddenly, I felt a sharp sting. I stood up and pulled off my flight suit as fast as I could, and saw a six-inch, menacing scorpion with a long, curly tail. I threw it off, screaming, "Get me out of here!" just as a jeep came by looking for me.

"What's your problem? I came as fast as I could," the sergeant yelled.

All I could do was point at my leg as I stood there in my underwear. I was too scared to be embarrassed. My leg throbbed like a second heartbeat.

The sergeant took one look at my blown-up thigh,

jumped out with a blanket, and lifted me into the jeep.

"What the heck?" he said, driving furiously to the base hospital.

Hyperventilating, I managed to say, "I think I got stung by a scorpion."

Lying in the hospital bed, I trembled, distraught about my swollen thigh and writhing in pain. I wept into my pillow and hoped there was some kind of medicine I could take so they wouldn't have to amputate my leg.

Chapter Twelve: May's Flight

At last, a doctor came in to visit me. The doctor tapped his stethoscope on his thin-framed chest. "Well, young lady, we'll give you a shot to bring the swelling down, but you can thank God that scorpion stings are not fatal during this time of year."

I turned my head away from the needle, dry swallowed, and closed my eyes. I almost felt reassured, but I was miserable with chills and almost cried once again. After he left, I turned my face into the hospital pillow and tried to sleep.

Hearing the door once more, I opened my eyes. Lana stood there, took one look at my leg, and said, "Hot damn, is that actually your leg? It looks like it has a twin!"

I restrained myself from laughing too hard, knowing it would cause more pain. "Thanks for coming by, Lana." I hugged her hard and didn't want to let go.

She released my embrace. "It's amazing you got to parachute again! This time you must join the Caterpillar Club."

"The what?" I smiled. Lana was the perfect dose of medicine I needed at a time like this, distracting me from my leg.

"Don't you know? In the 20s, the owner of a parachute company offered to give a gold pin to every person whose life was saved by one of his parachutes. The Army uses the Irvin Air Chute Company. I saw a pin that Audrey sent away for, after she had to jump from an AT-6 that went haywire." Lana sat on the edge of the hospital bed, trying to keep a distance from my swollen leg.

"What do they look like?" I said, squirming around, trying to get comfortable.

"They're darling! Each one is a two-inch, gold, curvy caterpillar with big ruby eyes. I wish I could get one." She showed me just how long with her red fingernails.

"I'll ask Audrey about it the next time I see her." *My brothers sure would get a kick out of me getting one,* I thought.

I was driven back to the base the next day, where I limped into the barracks toward my bed. There, in the middle of my bunk, was a jar with a large spider inside. Next to it was a handwritten sign that read: *Five cents to look at the scorpion that stung Violet.* On the blanket there lay 10 nickels. My bay mates were trying to capitalize on my hard luck! I laughed and laughed. Too bad they couldn't find a real scorpion.

It took about a week of lying around for my leg to heal. Getting a bill from the hospital added insult to my injury, reminding me once again that I was in the military, but not part of it. I soon felt quite useless and bored as I watched my bay mates come and go. I wrote another letter to Glenn, but then ripped it up, as he hadn't written back in months. I kept trying to reassure myself that it was because he was on a mission in the Pacific and couldn't send out mail.

After my leg was completely healed, I found a puppy wandering outside the barracks. I snuck the black-and-white mutt into my AT-11 for a ride. He looked a bit like my childhood dog, Blotchy, who had died a year earlier. He simply snuggled up to me and slept the whole flight. "Why, you brave little thing!" I cooed. Thoughts of Glenn, Blotchy and me up in his Jenny doing stunts made me heartsick. I missed our fulfilling conversations, and even more, the physical closeness of his arms wrapped around me.

After landing, I hid the puppy in my flight jacket. Once inside the barracks, I let him run around.

"He's adorable!" Adele giggled as she scooped him up and kissed him all over.

"What's his name, darlin'?" May asked, taking him from Adele.

I answered without hesitation, "Blotchy."

"Good name," said Mei-lee, trying to curl his tail.

All my bay mates fell in love with the puppy. It was challenging to sneak him food, and thank goodness there were no spot inspections. We were able to keep him a secret for a week, until he wandered off again after racking up over 40 hours in the air.

The following evening Adele and Mei-lee came into

the barracks.

"What's the matter, Mei-lee?" I stared at her almond-shaped eyes, which were now rounded into startled circles.

"Tell me, honey, what is it?" May folded her arm around Mei-lee's waist.

Adele interrupted, "Mei-lee ran out of fuel and had to land in a farmer's field."

Mei-lee took over the story. "A farmer chase me with pitch-fork, yelling, 'The Japs have landed, the Japs have landed.' Then I shout, 'I no Jap, I Chinese. Me Yankee girl pilot.'"

"Poor darlin'," May said, holding Mei-lee tighter.

Adele quickly added, "Townspeople came from all over the fields and surrounded her. A ranch hand pointed at her yelling, 'It's a Jap, all right.' Officer Pendleton told me he got a call from a cowboy saying there was a strange Japanese girl in the pasture and to come quick. Pendleton jumped out of his jeep and announced to the alarmed neighbors, 'This is one of our ferry pilots for the Army Airforces. Can't you folks see the Army insignia on her sleeve?'"

Mei-lee continued, wide-eyed. "Pendleton tell me, 'Hop in, Mei-lee, we get fuel for plane back at base.' I tell him, 'Sir, get me out here, go fast!'"

We all roared with laughter. Mei-lee joined in, happy the incident was over.

The following week I got the unfortunate assignment of chauffeuring around a colonel. Every once in a while we had to take non-flying male officers to other bases. They were often rude and made denigrating remarks. I met the colonel at the tarmac. He stood there with his huge belly protruding, his uniform covered with shiny medals.

He gave me the onceover and asked, "Are you really a pilot?"

I stood my ground. "Listen, get in or don't, I couldn't care less." I fussed with my coverall belt, then gazed up toward the dark clouds in the sky. He made a huffing noise, but got into the AT-18 anyway.

On this particular assignment I was to fly VIP Colonel Harlan back to his base. The only joy I got from it was that it was one hot plane! Prior to the flight, I had to memorize a three-page checklist, and master using an actual radio. It made the PT-19 Stearman seem slow. It had a closed canopy with a 1,200 horsepower engine, and a top speed of 272.

The weather started closing in on us. I was flying under low clouds and couldn't go higher than 13,000 feet without oxygen. Lightning flashed all around us.

The colonel asked, "Can't one of those lightning bolts

hit us?"

I confidently replied, "Don't worry, it never hits planes, especially not small ones, because there's nowhere for the lightning to ground." This boldfaced lie seemed to work, as he leaned back and began to nap. I knew I had better land soon. This storm was becoming bigger than I expected. Why oh why did the weather have to change when I was flying an important VIP? I spotted a little river, checked my map, and discovered an airport nearby.

When we landed, the colonel woke up with a disgusting snore, looked around, and bellowed, "You can't fool me, young lady! I know we're not in Texas. Don't think you're going to visit your boyfriend on my time."

I gathered up all my inner patience and calmly said, "I'm sorry, sir, the weather was just not cooperating today and for your safety I thought we had better land."

He gave me a stern military sneer. "Just point me to the Officers' Club."

After the weather cleared, I was glad to deposit the colonel in his proper place and head back to the base to do my *real* job.

The following day, I watched Lana go up in an open-cockpit airplane. I gave her a wave. I was doing a pre-flight check on a new, magnificent Curtiss C-46 transport plane nicknamed "the pregnant guppy" because of its large, wide-bodied cargo, when a white blouse fluttered by me on the tarmac. I looked up toward the sky, and saw

Lana buzzing me. Following above her appeared to be Lt. Huestis's plane.

"What the heck?" I said out loud. I was sure she would get washed right out of the program for buzzing me.

After she landed, I ran over to her plane. Before I could start my ranting and raving about the Army rules against flying too low, Lana began screaming from the cockpit.

"Hey, Violet, quick! Get me another shirt. I lost mine after I took it off to catch some sun." She frantically pointed at her brassiere.

"Lana, gosh darn you, you're going to get kicked right out of here if you don't stop breaking all the rules."

"God *damn* it, hurry up before Lieutenant Huestis comes flying overhead to gawk at me again!"

I ran back to the barracks, laughing all the way. Lana, sitting in her airplane in her underwear, was a sight to be seen. As I went past the bathroom, I saw two gals from another barracks soaping each other in the shower. I was so startled, I rushed into our room and grabbed one of my blouses. I heard loud giggling, then moaning. I darted out of there fast. On the way back to the tarmac I kept wondering, did I really see that? I had led a sheltered life, so I chose to believe that I didn't really hear those girls being intimate.

Lana, meanwhile, was sitting in her ship in her brassiere shouting, "Run faster!"

"Here." I threw the blouse at her, extremely annoyed.

Lana buttoned up the tight shirt, screaming, "This isn't mine."

"Oh, shut up and just put it on."

After Lana got out of her plane, we walked back to the mess hall together. I told her about the two girls in the shower.

"Those must be the gals from the N barracks; everyone's been talking about them." Lana pulled on the buttons of my blouse that she wore. "No wonder you grabbed the wrong shirt."

"They were really doing *that*?" I asked as my mouth hung open.

"Those lesbians better watch out. If the director gets wind of their escapades, they'll get washed right out of here before you can shout 'Fifinella.'"

"Speaking of getting washed out, you'd better stop your buzzing."

Exasperated, Lana said, "I had to buzz you, I needed a shirt!"

I didn't reply because I was busy reflecting. We certainly weren't allowed to do buzzing, and Lana had secretly told me she loved it. From time to time, she would fly so low over herds of cattle that it made them stampede and pile up on each other. She would brag about it to me later. I fretted that she might get kicked out for good if she kept up her crazy antics. If she did, I

143

would miss her dreadfully.

The following day, after hours of practicing maneuvers in the air, I marched back to the barracks. When I saw Lana come in an hour later, I couldn't help but burst out laughing.

"That was the funniest sight, seeing you sitting in your plane yesterday with only your brassiere on," I chuckled, then noticed the serious look on her face. "What's the matter?"

"Didn't you hear what happened to May?" Her eyes opened wide.

"No, what?"

"Ronnie, that hotshot pilot, started buzzing her, and before you knew it, both planes collided. May went down." Lana's hands flailed about in anger.

"Is she okay?" I asked nervously, biting the end of my braid.

"No," Lana said quietly.

I let out an uncontrollable sob, just as Adele burst in. "I was up there with her! All us gals were in formation following the rules of keeping 500 feet between planes, when that Ronnie boy moved closer. May was trying to maintain her course as he began to slow-roll around her plane. Apparently, he misjudged and his wing cut right through the cockpit canopy. I heard she died instantly." Adele looked solemnly toward the floor.

I tore myself away from all the commotion, threw

myself on the cot, and wept into my pillow. What a senseless death.

Lana came over and sat down beside me. "Violet, we can't let our emotions get away from us. There are men dying every day in battles. Besides, we're needed for our ferrying services. We shouldn't let one death stop us. Snap out of it! There's no time to mourn, we have work to do!"

I raised my head from the pillow. "Go away, Lana."

As Lana left, I let loose my sorrow. Being only 20 years old, I had never known anyone who had died. Lana was four years older than me, and had experienced more death than I had. I smothered my face farther into the pillow, thinking what a sweet, comforting friend May had been. Any time one of her bay mates had a problem, she was always there beside them with her soothing Southern ways.

Lana angrily banged her locker over and over again, which left me to think she was as upset as me. "God *damn* that showoff Ronnie," she screeched, shaking her fists and yelling at all our bay mates. "We all know he was hot-dogging, doing a roll over May's plane. I heard he's gotten demerits for buzzing the local school playground so low the children all had to run for cover."

"He only had 300 hours of flight time, but he had to show off to his buddies," Adele added.

"The Army's so-called investigation committee said it was just an accident, but we all know otherwise. I heard

Lieutenant Poxon say he had a momentary lapse in judgment and persuaded the committee not to even bother to investigate," Lana added hotly.

I sat up on my cot. "I might get over May's death eventually, but what steams me is I know that the WASPs probably won't even pay her funeral expenses. Director Cochran has still not convinced the general to make us part of the Army." I got up and stormed off to find someplace to be alone.

May's death proved to be a sobering experience, forcing all of us to look within to face our own mortality.

Posted all over the base the next day was the latest edition of the *Fifinella Gazette*:

May Cecilia Whitmore was the first woman ferry pilot to die on active duty. She was 23 years old, from Atlanta, Georgia, where her father is a storekeeper residing with her three younger siblings.

A collision caused the tip of the right wing of her plane to snap off. Nearby farmers heard the crash and came running to the site in the pasture.

Her BT-13 spun slowly down, rolling several times. It went into an inverted dive, rotating to the left and then slammed vertically into the ground. The plane plowed several feet into the soil and caught fire. Miss Whitmore's body was crushed upon impact.

Ronald Chessman was the cause of the accident. He will not be assigned blame, because the cause of the accident was deemed a momentary lapse of mental efficiency and general lack of alertness.

The funeral will take place next Saturday. A collection will be made to buy a coffin and assist the Whitmore family with funeral costs.

Found in her diary:

"I am always happier in the sky than on the ground, alone with the sun, the clouds, and the air."

KEEP 'EM FLYING, FIFINELLA

Flying in Formation

Later that week I was assigned to test an AT-17 Cessna Bobcat. It was by far the most expensive airplane designed for the Army. As I flew off in the $33,000 plane, I was more cautious than ever because of the recent accident.

I returned from my flight exhausted, and flopped on my cot thinking about the graduation ceremony the following week. First I lay on my stomach, arms tightly at my sides, hoping this would be the position that would send me into dreamland. I recalled my journey to this point—how frightening the train ride had been to Avenger Field, and the tears I tried to fight back when I left my family. Then I thought about the intensity of trying to pass the link trainer. My hands clenched as I remembered the black and blue marks on my legs after failing my first solo. Thinking of poor May again, I sadly curled up on my side. To seek the much needed sleep, I tried to remember all the good things that had happened to me during my six months of training—when Lana flew below my plane to guide me when I got lost; finding Blotchy to accompany me on a practice moonlight flight; all the laughing that poured out of me after the white glove inspections; the water fights, and the "scorpion" jar.

At last, I relaxed and let my body go, my eyes fluttering, my pigtails flying in the air, as I remembered Lana and Mei-lee throwing me into the reward of the cool wishing well.

That morning I awoke early, and sat quietly at our group's desk and reread the graduation flyer:

The 318th Army Airforces Flight Training Detachment announces the graduation of class 43-W-1, Friday December 17, 1943, Avenger Field, Sweetwater, Texas.

"I made it," I said out loud, then covered my mouth, realizing my bay mates were still asleep. I opened a letter from Emma that had arrived the day before.

Dear Violet:

Congratulations on your upcoming graduation. I received your invitation, but I cannot get a pass to leave. The front of the invitation is darling, with the embossed cartoon character. Is that your outfit's mascot?

Please accept the enclosed gift in my absence. I'm sure you'll hear from my sister Lolly. She recently moved to your parents' state with her two children because her husband joined the Navy.

Love, Cousin Emma

In the envelope was a $10 bill. *How very generous of her,* I thought.

Lana woke up with a loud yawn, startling me back to reality.

"Oh, Lana, I feel grand! We're really going to graduate. It's been a stressful six months, but well worth it!"

Lana fastened the zipper on her tailored blue skirt and arranged a wool beret around her rolling curls. "I'm glad to get rid of these damn zoot suits and put on the smart

Santiago Blues. Thank God Director Cochran talked the Army into issuing a decent uniform just in time for graduation, even though they did cost us a pretty penny."

I slipped on the dark blue "Ike" jacket and pinned up my pigtails inside the beret. "Lana, show me again how to knot the tie." I wanted to look perfect to impress my family. They were coming from very far away for the graduation. I wondered how Mother would react to my new uniform.

Chapter Thirteen: Graduation

Graduation day finally arrived. As Director Jacqueline Cochran entered the administration building, all the WASPs, including their families, applauded loudly from the bleachers. She twirled around, gave a curtsey, and tipped her new blue beret.

"Girls, you all look sensational in your well-deserved uniforms. It was worth my money to hire a professional model and designer to get the general's approval." She winked at General Arnold, who nodded in return. "As you go on to further assignments, these uniforms will provide you with the respect you deserve. I would like to welcome family and friends to the first graduating class of the Women Airforce Service Pilots.

"Ladies, you have the honor and distinction of being the first women pilots trained by the Army. You have demonstrated your value, even though the WASPs are still regarded as an experiment. I need you to go forth and continue to prove your merit. At least 750 pilots are needed by the end of the year, so the WASP program will continue to expand!"

The audience burst into thunderous applause.

"Pilots, you have successfully completed 55 hours in Primary Trainers, 65 hours in basics, and 38 hours of instrument flying, as well as 60 hours in the advanced trainers. The general and I are proud of your accomplishments. Some of your classmates have sadly washed out. You are the women with the tenacity and perseverance to have made it—only 23 out of a class of 30. The Army is very satisfied with your successes. We hope you will continue the pace by going onward to Pursuit or Bomber school, or one of the other advanced assignments. Before you receive your engraved graduation wings, let us bow our heads in prayer for the soul of May Cecilia Whitmore, who bravely died in service for our country."

Everyone bowed their heads. Crossing myself as tears dripped down my face, I found a lace hanky in my pocket to sniffle into. I felt guilty that May was not with us, and looked out a window at the expansive Texas sky, praying she was joyfully free-flying up there…somewhere.

Director Cochran continued, "These silver wings have a lozenge in the middle, representing the shield of Athena, the goddess of war and wisdom. May it bring you all the courage to continue to serve our great country. Lana Walton, please step forward." The director pinned the sparkling wings on Lana's broad-collared uniform.

Lana stood proudly, smiling at us while shaking the director's hand.

I was next. A tingling sensation moved up my body after I shook both the director's hand and the general's. I felt the smooth silver wings, traced over the 43-W-1 on my crisp new uniform, giving me a blissful feeling of accomplishment, elated to have been the first 1943 WASP class to graduate.

After we received our wings, our names were put in Director Cochran's beret as the general drew one name out. "Violet Willey," he announced.

I gasped. Little ole me would be co-piloting with the famous Jacqueline Cochran to Washington, D.C.!

I rushed over to my family, hoping they had seen me receive my wings and being picked the winner. I saw Mother, Dad, and my cousin Lolly, and wondered where my brothers were.

Dad came toward me. "Congratulations on winning the co-piloting with Director Cochran. Honey, I'm proud of you. I'm sure you'll do great in Pursuit School and learn how to get those fighters to our men to win this war!"

"Thanks for all your support, Dad. I missed you so much!" I gave him a big hug as tears came to my eyes.

He held me tight and kissed me on the cheek. "Mrs. Conney came by yesterday and gave us a letter she received from Glenn to give to you. She also said to say congratulations." Dad handed me an envelope.

"That was sweet of her. I haven't heard from Glenn in a long time." I clutched the letter.

Mother gave me a stilted hug. "It's lucky that you graduated."

It was more than luck, I thought, but I did not want to pursue an argument in front of the family, and simply said, "Thanks. Where are the boys?"

Cousin Lolly heard me through the crowd. "They're over there, playing hide-and-go-seek in the bleachers with my children."

"Hi, Lolly! It was nice of you to come to my graduation." I gave her a peck on the cheek.

"I was happy to make it. Besides, it helps pass the time waiting for my husband to come home from the Navy. You look all grown up in that stylish uniform."

"Thanks," I said, straightening my tie.

"I brought you a little present." She reached inside her plaid coat and gave me a little white box. Inside, on a bed of cotton, were two pearl earrings.

"They're lovely. Thanks, Lolly!"

"I knew your mother gave you the necklace when you first joined the WASPs. My mom gave me the pearl earrings when I got married, but I'd really like you to have the matching set."

After embracing her, I fastened the earrings on and twirled the necklace. "Thank you, thank you!" I held out one of my ear lobes, while tilting my head at her.

"You're very welcome. I'm sure they'll be a wonderful lucky charm for you when you're thousands of feet up in the air." She smiled brightly.

After I saw my family off on the train, I felt melancholy that Glenn wasn't with me to share the excitement of my graduation. I reassured myself that this was all part of being in wartime. Everyone had a job to do. I knew it would be over soon enough, and then we could share our experiences without any distance between us. Sad to see my family leave, I waved goodbye to everyone. Tommy and Howie stuck their tongues out at me through the train window, making me chuckle. My bad mood dissipated. I returned the tongue gesture, and went back to the barracks to freshen up for our graduation party. I was happy to have a few minutes to read Glenn's letter. I sat at the study table and opened the envelope.

Dear Dad and Mom:

I am not sure if you will get this letter or how much of it will be coherent because of all the censoring. I barely have enough time to write this. Please tell Violet's parents that I am doing fine, then they can write to her for me.

I feel very valuable being chosen for the Marine squadron F-11 Grumman Wildcat fighters, since there are only 12 of us. Wake Island is a strange place, as the entire island is only five miles long and four miles wide.

There is a severe lack of supplies. Many parts of the big guns are missing. We all know that being in the Pacific is definitely the place to keep an eye out for the Japanese.

Yesterday they swooped down with three squadrons of 36 bombers. We were taken by surprise as they came in very low and fast. Two of the 12 wildcats were destroyed within a matter of seconds. Thank God we were able to shoot down a few Japanese bombers, even though there are now only 10 of us left! We did patch up two fighters from yesterday's assault. Major Devereux anticipates another attack tomorrow.

Well, sorry this is short but I must get some shut-eye.

Please keep me in your prayers,

Your son, Glenn

His letter left me feeling very troubled. Our future together seemed shaky. I had never really grasped the true concept of the war. Now, it was coming close to home for me with my beloved in the grip of overseas fighting.

That night at the hotel ballroom, the starched-white tablecloths capped with extravagant bottles of champagne in buckets of ice astounded me. I folded my new uniform skirt under as I sat down. "Lana, the orchestra is grand!"

Lana leaned over to me and whispered, "Not only am I thrilled to have graduated, but I got away with dating Gus the whole time!" She looked up and there he was with his dashing smile, asking her for a dance.

Mei-lee, Adele, and I drank as much champagne as we could, toasting to Fifinella while rehashing stories about our adventures during basic training.

Adele reminisced, "Remember when I tried out my first test plane, the AT-6 Texan? I did the usual routine check before taking off, flew to 11,000 feet, and then I entered a spin. When I tried to pull out of it, the rotation wouldn't pick up speed despite my efforts. Finally, I reversed all the usual inputs and pulled out only 500 feet above the ground. After landing, I discovered that Johnny the mechanic had mistakenly hooked up all the controls backwards." Adele laughed so hard her beret slid off her busy hair.

"I remember it well," I said. "But at the time we all didn't find it that funny."

"You right," Mei-lee agreed. "Remember when gas main broke, we very cold, we got up, put on flight gear, went back to sleep under blankets?"

"That was a hoot. It made us go to Sweetwater and buy those God-awful red long johns from the store," Adele added.

"And we bought cowboy boots after picking up six-inch mudpacks on our oxfords from the squishy, gluey Texas mud," I said a little too loudly, realizing how much champagne I had drunk.

The clarinet seemed to be laughing along with us as the piano tickled me. The big band music lifted our euphoria higher and higher. Too bad it was getting so late. I had to get up early for my flight with the director. When they played "String of Pearls," I thought I had died and gone to Heaven. I left the girls, satisfied my favorite song had been played, and strolled back to the barracks for some shut-eye.

The next morning I met Director Cochran in her office. I had the jitters because of being the one chosen to fly her back to Washington. I followed her out to her beautiful twin-engine Cessna.

The director took a moment and studied the clouds. "Ahh, the wonderful cirrus clouds. Good weather for us!"

I looked up at the sky and was glad I had done well in meteorology class. I was able to recognize the white mare's tails of the cirrus clouds. I got into the Cessna with confidence, knowing I would be a competent co-pilot for

Mrs. Cochran.

"I'm happy to be your co-pilot to Washington, Director. Thank you." I smiled and quivered with anticipation.

"You're more than welcome, Violet. That was a wonderful graduation ceremony. I'm feeling very confident about all the incoming classes that will be needed to serve our country." The director looked over the controls as I carefully taxied down the runway. Much to my relief, the takeoff was near perfect.

About an hour later, the small Cessna rattled as we entered a stretch of rough air.

"Damn, altocumulus clouds are starting to form!" the director said.

Sure enough, the grayish clouds, some darker than others, gave us the warning that thunderstorms were brewing. I tapped the wheel anxiously with my fingers and hoped the weather would change back to beautiful as fast as it had become uncertain. Director Cochran looked surprised as this unexpected electrical storm caused all the flight instruments to go crazy.

"Violet, what position are we in?" she shouted.

"I'm afraid I have no idea," I replied meekly, feeling shaken and disappointed that my trip with the legendary aviatrix was not turning out as I had imagined. My pounding hangover from the champagne the night before didn't help the matter any.

The director tried to help me find a hole in the storm clouds, but the changing course of the plane made it impossible to keep track of our position. All I knew was the gas gauge was low and we had better land, no matter where we were. I peered at the gauge one more time, and then at Director Cochran. The look in her eyes told me she knew this. I kept clutching my pearl necklace while murmuring a steady prayer.

"Violet, I can see a pasture. Land over there. "

We bounced over the grass and we skidded toward a ditch. I was able to stop, but the plane wrapped around a barbed wire fence. Sweat sopped the collar of my jacket.

Jacqueline Cochran quickly got on the radio to the nearest air control center. "This is N89210. Send help. We are somewhere in Kentucky. Just get out, Violet."

I was still shaking. I had to crawl through the fence to get out to the pasture, while Director Cochran remained on the radio inside. I held myself, trying not to shiver and save face in front of her, but the director didn't pay attention to me after getting out. She stood there staring out into the vast distance, waiting for something.

Darkness was closing in as fast as the rain came. I blinked back tears and continued to hug myself for warmth.

After an hour of silent shivering, a limousine appeared across the field and headed straight toward us. I was so surprised by the size of the car that I didn't realize I was lamely standing in the pouring rain.

Mrs. Cochran simply straightened her uniform as she entered the huge vehicle and shouted, "Hurry up, Violet, get in! Well, Colonel, thank you for accommodating us," she said to a man inside the car.

"My pleasure, Director, my home is your home. This weather's mighty nasty. The reports say it should clear by tomorrow."

When we reached our destination and got out, my eyes were drawn upward to the multiple, tall white columns and the long black shutters adorning every window. The colonel's Kentucky home was elegant.

Inside, an elderly Negro maid escorted me up a cascading staircase that reminded me of my favorite movie, *Gone With the Wind*. I felt like a kid at Christmas as we passed room after room. The maid stopped at the end of the grand hallway.

"This is your room, madam."

"Thank you," I said in a small voice as she quickly disappeared.

The chairs in my room wore decorative dresses. I touched the soft, fuzzy texture of the wallpaper, which was embossed with raised, scarlet-colored paisley flowers made of felt. Then, my eyes landed on the fireplace. A fireplace in a bedroom! There were only two in our farmhouse — one in the living room and one in the dining room.

On the finely webbed, crocheted bedspread was a beige, lace-trimmed cotton flannel nightgown.

161

The four-poster canopied bed had long, sheer curtains surrounding it, pulled back with woven gold braids. I undressed, folded my damp uniform on one of the fancy chairs, pulled on the lovely scented gown and laid my head on the pillow. *Ah, civilization – sleeping in a real bed.* I immediately fell off to slumberland, the memory of the exhausting flight fading away.

The next morning, I awoke to aromas that I had not smelled in a long time. I put on my wrinkled uniform, then washed my face in a huge, elegant bathroom down the hall. I stepped down the winding staircase, feeling quite glorious after a good night's sleep in a huge feather bed. In the dining room, the chandelier above the grand cherry dining table was similar to the one in the hotel in Houston, but on a smaller scale.

At the breakfast table, the colonel and Director Cochran were discussing the war. I cheerfully said good morning. They acknowledged me briefly and went back to their conversation.

"Thank God the invasion of Italy is over," Director Cochran said, then took a dainty sip of her tea.

"General Patton's troops evacuated 39,000 Germans and restored Sicily to its citizens," the colonel said with great satisfaction.

I was happy to not be included in the conversation as I took in the feast before me. The so-called breakfast looked more like a dinner. There was a whole ham on a tiny, flower-bordered platter, scrambled eggs in an oval-shaped porcelain bowl, pitchers of milk and apple juice, big stacks of buckwheat cakes with a cup of syrup, and a large plate of butter. Butter had become scarce since the war began, and I was quite surprised to see it. There was so much food it made me wonder if the colonel even had to use ration coupons. As I listened to the conversation, I heard the colonel correcting Director Cochran.

"You mean Colonel Hobby, don't you, Jackie?" he said, straightening out his mustache.

"Yes, I suppose you could call Mrs. Hobby a colonel," she said with a smug smile.

I hadn't eaten such rich food in over six months. The ham was far superior to the Spam at the mess hall, as were the real eggs over the powdered ones. The crispy, crunchy hash brown potato cakes were a far cry from the soggy, mushy instant mashed potato mess at the base. I never did adjust to Army food.

The flight to Washington, D.C., was smooth sailing, and I got to know the director better. She sat at the controls next to me humming a Cole Porter song, "I Get a Kick Out of You." As I grew more comfortable in her presence, I felt bold enough to ask her the question that was always on the minds of many the WASPs. "Why aren't we part of the Army, Director?" I asked timidly.

"The WASPs are not part of the Army because Mrs. Hobby is head of the Women's division," Director Cochran answered curtly.

I made myself continue on, even though I knew Mrs.

Hobby was really supposed to be addressed as a colonel. "Couldn't the WASPs be a part of the WAACs in order to get Army benefits?"

"I will tell you something privately, Violet. Mrs. Hobby doesn't know the tail of an airplane from the nose. Why, once when I attempted to discuss aeronautics, she responded by telling me her seven-year-old son loved airplanes and had them on the wallpaper in his bedroom!" She burst out laughing, while keeping her eyes on the instruments.

"Oh." I tried to understand her point. "It never bothered me to just have Civil Service status until May died and we all had to chip in for her funeral expenses."

"Look, Violet, I know how you all feel and I feel the same way, which is why I have written a bill to present to Congress. I want the WASPs to be part of the Army Airforces and not part of the WAACs," Director Cochran said.

"Thank you for explaining this to me."

Director Cochran simply looked out the Cessna's tiny window and hummed another Cole Porter song.

I left the Director in Washington, and then headed to the Pursuit School in Palm Springs. It was a hard contrast to be back in a barracks sleeping on a cot, rather than in that wonderful, heavenly bed at the colonel's. I was honored to have been one of the few accepted into Pursuit School, but I hoped I was big and strong enough to handle such powerful planes.

Jacqueline Cochran, with a P-51 Mustang

Chapter Fourteen: Pursuit School

Dear Dad and Mother:

I am proud to be in Pursuit School, and I should be able to visit you now that I am stationed in Palm Springs, California. I find the weather more tolerable than the suffocating West Texas air. Palm Springs is hot (102 midday) but it is a pleasant, dry heat. Texas always had thunder and lightning this time of year, which swayed the barracks. Here, we are lucky to get a maximum of only 15-20 days of rain.

Pursuits are the new fighter planes just developed for the Army. They are designed for only one pilot to fly alongside bomber airplanes to protect them from the enemy. Pursuit School is only four weeks long. We learn to fly the planes and are drilled on emergency procedures.

I am quite honored to fly these small, maneuverable, super-fast, advanced piston engine fighter airplanes. I should get a leave after this training session is over; then I'll take a train and come to visit you.

Give the boys my love, Violet

I sealed the letter and marched off to my first class.

Instructor Reynolds showed us a film on how to handle a fighter plane if the engine fails in midair.

"Pursuits have three times the accident rate of any previous airplanes that you're used to. Always leave the runway at full throttle. If the engine ever fails, simply land it like a glider," he lectured. "I would now like to introduce you to Mr. Marshall, a Bell Factory representative for the newly designed P-47 Thunderbolt."

Instructor Reynolds looked out of date in his 1930's gabardine suit and tie, compared to Mr. Marshall, who wore a stylish, double-breasted suit with a plaid bow tie.

Mr. Marshall scanned the room of over 50 of us WASPs. "Thank you, Mr. Reynolds. Ladies, I have a great respect for your ability to help in the war effort. We honor your intelligence to learn all about our Pursuits in order to get them to our men in combat."

We all started clapping for ourselves. Mr. Reynolds smiled broadly and commenced with his lecture as he adjusted his bow tie. "The specs on this aircraft are as follows: it has a 36-foot-long wingspan, 14 feet 8 inches in height, its speed is 433 MPH, with a service ceiling of 43,000 feet and a ferry range of 1,800 miles. By the way, it cost the Army $85,000 to manufacture it."

I could barely keep from whistling. My God, the Jenny, the Piper Cub, the PT-19, even the AT-17 barely compared to the speed of the Pursuit. Excitement rushed through my body as I thought about flying the fastest airplane ever made.

A few weeks later, I was glad to run into one of my old bay mates, Myrna, from basic training. I had seen her in class, but never got a chance to say hello.

"Hi, Violet, I see you're still wearing those pigtails."

"I find it practical. Helps keep the hair out of my eyes."

Myrna was a 22-year-old widow. After losing her husband in the war she had joined the WASPs out of a need to serve her country. I admired her ability to make the most out of her life after experiencing such a loss.

"Myrna, did you get issued your .45 yet?" I asked.

"I did. The Army sure is serious about protecting the design of the Pursuits from enemies. What have you been up to lately?" Myrna looked down at the floor as she pulled a black ribbon tighter around her dark-brown bun.

She appeared older than everyone and hadn't attracted much attention from any of our male instructors when we were in basic training. Myrna rarely made direct eye contact or smiled.

"I just received an assignment to test the P-47," I said proudly.

"Lucky you. That's the most high-powered Pursuit plane ever built," Myrna replied, looking out at the row of Pursuits glistening in the sunshine.

"I feel very honored that the Army is trusting me to fly it." I moved my head, trying to catch her eye.

"When are you going?"

"After I finish the last class, in two weeks." I gave up on getting her to look me in the eye.

"Let me know how the Thunderbolt handles when you get back. I've always wondered," Myrna said.

"I sure will. Nice to see you again, Myrna. It's almost time for mail call. Want to come with me?"

"I have a lot of studying to do." She turned and headed toward the barracks.

She probably doesn't get much mail, I thought sadly. I, however, received a letter from Lana:

Dear Violet:

Towing target sleeves for the gunnery crews has proved to be quite thrilling and it really stretches my skill as a pilot. Every day I fly an A-24 with a 30-foot-long muslin sleeve at the end of 1,500 feet of steel cable. Army soldiers on the ground shoot off round after round of gunfire at the long piece of cloth that trails behind me. This is the best way for the soldiers to practice their firing. I really enjoy working with these two privates, Arnie and Lee. They are a gas! Arnie shoots yellow, wax-covered bullets and Lee shoots blue. After they signal me down they count the colored holes in the sleeve and pony up bets to see who shot the most! They are very complimentary about my flying and I love doing it. Arnie especially is a hot looker, with short, brown wavy hair and thick eyebrows, and the dreamiest blue eyes. It's his smile that really gets to me.

The other day I was beginning to feel very confident in my flying ability, keeping my eyes straight ahead, knowing one wrong turn and I could be shot at, when I felt a burning sensation in my foot. I made an emergency landing after realizing a bullet had caught my left big toe.

The crew (which did not include Arnie and Lee this time) rode out to where I landed and started screaming at me, "Why the hell did you land that suddenly, Lana?"

I shrieked back at all of them, "You shot my goddamned toe, you idiots!"

They were pretty quiet as they helped me hobble into the jeep, then drove me off to the infirmary. I had the medic save the bullet and was able to get a local jeweler to make a necklace out of it!

I know you won't believe me, Violet, but I'm actually allowed to do buzzing on this job. I buzz over the soldiers to spray tear gas on them. This gives the troops practice on how fast they can snap on their gas masks. It gives me such a kick to watch them scramble!

Tonight will be my first tow targeting flight at night, with the gunnery crews using searchlights.

Write me back soon and wish me luck!

I sure miss you, kid! Lana

P.S. After I get tired of tow targeting, I was thinking of applying to Pursuit School. I sorely miss you and my ole buddies from Avenger.

Tow Targeting

That Lana is such a pistol, I thought. Aching to rekindle the close friendship we had shared, I wrote back to her immediately.

Dear Lana:

I miss you a lot. I found it frightening to read about your tow targeting experiences.

I know this is the best way for the soldiers to learn to shoot a flying target before they go overseas. I really admire your guts, but please be careful, as I wouldn't want to lose you.

I'm back in the classroom in the middle of four weeks of Pursuit School. When I'm not in class, all I do is study. I miss my life in the sky, but feel proud that I will be able to ferry the fighter planes from the factories to the bases for the troops real soon.

I got a letter from Mei-lee. She is helping design a "relief tube" for women with Dr. Ethel Grace. A model was made of a workable design, which included crotch zippers because of the problem with women's underwear. Then she flew a different plane every day with a variety of clothing to be tested. In another experiment, the doctor covered her body with thermocouples that would record her temperature. She walked in mud, then climbed on the wing to see if the traction was good. Mei-lee doesn't seem very happy with her assignment. She has put in a request to attend Pursuit School and wrote me saying she is quite sick of her clothing-testing career!

I do love the weather in Palm Springs and don't miss the nasty climate in Texas one bit.

I have written my fiancé, Glenn, several letters and they just keep coming back "undeliverable." I hope he is all right. Please keep him in your prayers.

Must hurry off to class, and be careful!

Miss you sorely, Violet

P.S. I hope you get accepted into Pursuit School. I will probably be done by the time you get here, but maybe we can go on some adventures together later!

I did so well in my classes that I was given the privilege to be the first one up in the P-47 Thunderbolt. As

I gained altitude, the landmarks got smaller and smaller below me. Oh, this plane was a honey! It was empowering to be the first woman to test this type of airplane. My engine hummed as I happily climbed upwards. It seemed as though all I had to do was *think* "right" and it would turn right. I was flying along in a fighter plane, at last! The sheer exhilaration made me feel heavenly as I climbed among the scattered cotton and cream-colored clouds. It was hard to believe that just a few years ago the only plane I had access to was a Curtiss Jenny. Glenn Miller's "String of Pearls" was floating within my head as I tapped out the rhythm with my fingers on the wheel.

Suddenly, the controls jammed. I was sure this plane had been in the repair shop several times. It seemed to be displaying the erratic behavior the mechanics had noted, but had supposedly fixed. Unable to control it, I went into a dive. Should I parachute out and let $85,000 worth of airplane crash? I could not bring myself to destroy this beautiful flying machine. I had to make the most serious decision of my life—to bail or not to bail? My hands trembled as I contemplated landing this uncontrollable machine.

As I descended, I was able to recover the plane from the dive only a few hundred feet from the ground, and had enough control movement to land. Rolling to a stop, I released my throbbing grip on the controls. Then, I regained enough confidence to call back to the base to be picked up. After rethinking what had just happened, I realized that I certainly was not to blame for the failure of the Pursuit. After all, I was merely a test pilot, and test it I did, and it did not pass! I recalled Instructor Reynolds saying that most of the fighter planes were so new they went from the drawing board to the flight line in only six months. Thank God (and Fifinella) that I was not killed, and the expensive Pursuit landed in one piece. I sat back and tried to relax while I waited for help.

One of the nicer mechanics was sent to pick me up, and we had a good conversation on the way back to the base.

Once back inside the barracks, I saw Adele.

"Hi, Adele. Were you able to pick up my mail for me today?"

"Yes, Violet, you got a letter," she said, and pulled it out of her locker.

I sat on my cot and read the letter from my mother.

"Oh, my God!" I gasped.

"What's the matter?" Adele asked.

"My Glenn was shot and killed on Wake Island, this, this…" I could barely form the words. "…is why I haven't heard from him…"

Adele exclaimed, "Oh, no…" and embraced me.

I broke away from her. I threw my face into my pillow, letting loose my tears. An agonizing animal noise came from deep within my body. My greatest fear had come true as to why Glenn had not written. I wrapped myself in the blankets and curled into a fetal position, rocking back and forth, saying, "Lord, surround and protect me," over and over again. I fell asleep briefly, sucking on one of my braids.

After a restless night, I couldn't function. I knew I could get away with being taken off the flight schedule by saying that I had my period, since the flight surgeon still wanted any of the WASPs grounded during "that time of the month." I found Adele in the mess hall and asked her to get me off the schedule for a few days, then went back to the barracks. I had a severe, pounding headache, and stayed in bed for three days, though it felt more like a month. On the fourth day I was able to take a long, hot shower, since everyone was out flying or in class. I wrapped a towel around my body and one on my head, then wrote Lana a letter.

Dear Lana:

My Glenn is gone. I guess he leaves this earth as a hero, and I am proud to say this, but I am also full of sorrow. I had it in my heart that we would return from our war duties, get married, and start a family.

I wish you were here to tell me to snap out of my blue mood and get back to work to help win this God-awful war.

I took most of the week off under the guise of having my period. This way I can save my leave time for the funeral.

Sadly, Violet

I was able to request a leave for the funeral. I packed a few of my civilian clothes and headed to catch a bus to get to the train station. On the ride home, I dozed off and on in a daze. Waiting for a bus from the train station to home, I tried to prepare myself for when I saw my mother. Would she comfort me, or chastise me to be strong and brave? The bus dropped me off a mile away from home. As I walked, my suitcase became heavier and heavier the closer I got. The farmhouse came into view. It appeared much smaller to me now. My mind went back to the wondrous plantation I had stayed in with the director. I had only been gone from home for a year, but it seemed much longer. Walking in the front door, I was careful not to bang the screen, which Dad had still not fixed.

"Hello, Mother," I said going into the kitchen and giving her a hug. She returned the hug stiffly, but I wasn't surprised. I knew she missed me, even though she was unable to show affection.

"Nice to see you, Violet, even though it's under difficult circumstances." She returned to peeling apples for a pie.

"I still can't even believe my Glenn is gone..." I looked down at the worn kitchen floor, a tear escaping my eye. "I'll help you with that," I said, after Mother didn't respond to my grief.

"Thanks, dear. I'll finish rolling out the top crust if you could slice the apples."

I slowly cut each apple, starting to feel sad again, then anxious about the upcoming funeral. Howie and Tommy ran in, chasing around me and poking at each other.

"Boys, stop your shenanigans and give your big sister a hug," Mother commanded. They gave me a quick squeeze, then ran out the back door just when I was about to ask Tommy how his paper route was doing.

"Where is Dad, Mother?"

"Out in the back 40, pruning."

"I missed you both," I said, longing for more affection.

"Yes, dear," she said. "We missed you, too." She turned away from me and retrieved a bag of sugar from the cupboard.

I heard the door slam and saw Dad, looking tired, as well as older. His face brightened as soon as he saw me. "My Vi-Vi, how I've missed you!" He hugged me firmly. As his strong arms wrapped around me, my dammed-up tears cascaded down my face.

"I'm so very sorry, Violet. I really liked Glenn, and I pictured you two as a really special couple."

I couldn't stop sobbing. I glanced up and saw Mother giving me a sympathetic look. I broke from Dad's embrace and went into the bathroom. Running cold water in the sink and splashing it on my cheeks, I pulled myself together, praying, "Lord, protect and surround me. Fifinella stay on my shoulder." This silly prayer, the one I used every time I flew an Army Pursuit, gave me the courage to go back to the kitchen. I wiped the leftover scraps of piecrust from the counter, cleaning the surface as Mother put the apple pie in the oven. The sound of the Zenith and the smell of Dad's cigar gave me a safe, secure, homey feeling. I realized that Mother had made the pie just for me and the sugar must have taken many ration coupons. I tried to put on my best face as I helped her set the table for dinner.

I awoke that night from a terrible nightmare. I found it amazing how the mind could throw puzzle pieces of one's life into a scene that really didn't fit together. I dreamed May had married my Glenn, and they had soared up into the sky in a B-29 for their honeymoon. Just as they reached altitude, the plane blew up, shaking me awake.

Chapter Fifteen: The Medal of Honor — Hop-Scotching Across the Country

I took a hot bath before anyone in the family would need the bathroom. Soaking in the big iron claw-foot tub was soothing to my aching body. I hadn't been able to treat myself to a bath for more than a year. I lay in the water, thinking, *Pull yourself together; you can get through this funeral. If you can risk your life flying Pursuits, certainly you can do this.* I had decided to pack my Santiago Blues to wear in honor of Glenn at the funeral.

It was a week-long, arduous train ride to Arlington National Cemetery. Soldiers usually gave up their seats for Mother, but many times Dad, the boys, and I had to sit on our suitcases. Sometimes we got to go to bed in a sleeper; other times it was just too full, with all the troops traveling to bases.

Glenn had been awarded a medal of honor, which entitled him to a full military burial. We walked to the gravesite on the perfectly trimmed green lawn surrounded by well-placed maple trees. Anger built inside me as hundreds of evenly placed gravestones came into view. I unconsciously reached into my uniform, grabbed for my pearls, and twisted them on my neck, nearly choking myself. Mother glanced back to look at me as I started coughing. Embarrassed, I tucked them back in my blouse. Looking around, I saw some of the same neighbors that were at my going-away party when I left for the WASPs. Instead of their gay attire, everyone wore somber black, as if they were trying to blend into the shadows of the trees. Why couldn't this be a gathering for our wedding, instead of my beloved's funeral?

The Marine Funeral Band played ruffles on the drums and flourishes on the bugle, adding to the atmosphere of sadness as they marched by us. Following close behind was the symbolic caparisoned riderless horse. The sight of the horse caused Mrs. Conney to cover a cry into her flowered hanky, which made me cover my own mouth to prevent a sob from escaping. Several Marines carrying rifles marched past, followed by the flag bearers. Mr. and Mrs. Conney fell into the line as they nodded for me to follow with my family.

On a small table surrounded by hundreds of marble gravestones lay a helmet and an M-1 rifle, signifying that Glenn's remains had been unable to be transported back from Wake Island.

Monsignor Monahan, wearing his long black frock, presided before us saying the familiar Latin prayers. I answered at the appropriate times along with everyone else, feeling a single moment of comfort lost in the familiarity of the ceremony. The Marine riflemen marched in precision and shot off three rounds, jolting me back to a dark cloud of reality. The bugler played the slow melancholy "Taps." Mrs. Conney wailed, which gave me the freedom to join her. Six white-gloved Marines ceremoniously folded the Stars and Stripes, carefully ending with the 48 stars showing in the proper triangle. After presenting it to Mrs. Conney, the Marines stepped back and saluted. Mrs. Conney reached for my hand and placed it on the flag with hers. This time I kept my emotions in check, receiving Mrs. Conney's gift of comfort.

General Taylor stood before us and read the official award: "The United States Marine Corps hereby presents a Medal of Honor to Glenn William Conney for conspicuous gallantry, intrepidity at the risk of his life above and beyond the call of duty while attached to Marine Fighter Squadron 207, during action against enemy Japanese land, surface, and aerial units at Wake Island. Engaging vastly superior forces of enemy bombers and warships, Captain Glenn Conney shot down two of a flight of 23 hostile planes, executing repeated bombing and strafing runs at extremely low altitude and close range, and succeeded in inflicting deadly damage upon a large Japanese vessel, thereby sinking the first major warship to be destroyed by small-caliber bombs delivered from a fighter-type aircraft. When his plane was disabled by hostile fire and no other ships were operative, Captain Conney landed and assumed command of one flank of the line set up in defiance of the enemy. And, conducting a brilliant defense enabled his men to hold their positions and repulse determined Japanese attacks, repeatedly proceeding through intense hostility to provide covering fire for unarmed ammunition carriers. Responsible in a large measure for the strength of his sector's gallant resistance, Captain Conney led his men with bold aggressiveness until he was mortally wounded. His superb skill as a pilot, daring leadership, and unswerving devotion to duty distinguished him among the defenders of Wake Island, and his valiant conduct reflects the highest credit upon himself and the United States Naval Service. He gallantly gave his life for his country."

The general held out a red-white-and-blue-striped ribbon with an attached bronze medal. The medal was in the shape of a finely crafted airplane propeller. Mr. Conney received it, holding it firmly to his chest as the general saluted.

Grief stricken, I looked into Mr. Conney's sad face. The color of his eyes mirrored Glenn's, causing a longing in my heart.

After the long trip back home, I lay in my childhood bed. I overheard my parents talking in the living room.

"It's a shame that his body was never recovered and Glenn didn't have a nice burial casket," Mother said.

"Yes, Martha, I suppose it would have been nice to have seen a flag-draped military casket, but I'm afraid my mind has been on the fact that Violet can't share her life with Glenn now. I was even picturing what our grandchildren would have looked like when we were at the funeral."

After hearing this, I put my head under my pillow and cried and cried until I could cry no more, eventually falling asleep from exhaustion.

Shortly after returning back to the base, I attended a mandatory meeting in the barracks. Hazel, the assigned leader, called the WASPs together and announced, "Girls, as your squadron leader, I need you to continue to inform the flight surgeon when your next menstrual period is due, because we have been ordered not to fly during our menstrual cycles. Especially on high-altitude missions." She shifted uncomfortably as she spoke.

Adele was the first to react to this irritating bit of news. "That's none of the flight surgeon's business, nor anyone's, for that matter, but my own!" She shook her busy hair about in anger adding, "It's none of their beeswax!"

"I'm sorry, girls. I'm under orders to have you report this because fainting or weakness can occur during the duress of menses," Hazel stated with obvious uncertainty, as if reading a script.

"Forewarned is forearmed," Adele mumbled as her eyes narrowed.

I clenched my teeth, sick and tired of Adele's stupid old sayings. I was still too full of grief at the loss of my love to find the energy to lash out at her. I agreed that grounding us during our menstrual periods was ridiculous and impossible to enforce.

When all the girls marched back to the bay after chow that night, they cut loose with a griping session. The WASPs in our bay (just as in the other bays) came to the conclusion that everyone had very irregular periods due to flying, making their cycles unpredictable. We all decided to lie about them, since all we cared about was flying to win this war, and didn't wish to be grounded under any circumstances. I felt uncomfortable, and even guilty, that I had used the excuse of having my period to get the time off to grieve for Glenn.

The next day, Adele and I checked the board to see when or if we were flying that day. Mei-lee, who had been accepted into Pursuit School and now joined us in Palm Springs, peered behind us. I was happy that her job of testing clothing was over.

"Hey, WASPIES, we on schedule today."

"Looks like I get another 'widow-maker' because of the nine-week course I took on it in Kansas," Adele sighed.

"At least it's not one of the unreliable planes like the Bunsen burners, flying coffins, or buckets of bolts. Thanks to you and some of the other WASPs, the male pilots are not afraid to fly the widow-makers anymore," I replied.

"I found that the engine would catch on fire, but I still could land it safely," Adele said, now looking proud as she straightened the wings on her uniform. "The mechanics worked out the problem and the pilots realized it wasn't such a beast after all. The other day, I overheard them saying, 'If a girl can fly it, we can, too.'" Adele did a good imitation of a male voice.

Adele was such a whiz kid. I did envy her quick ability to absorb all the information that was constantly thrown at us about all the different airplanes. She was even beginning to look smarter, now tying her wild hair back with a pretty barrette. I reflected on how moody I was feeling, as my thoughts bounced about from annoyance toward Adele to admiration, all in a matter of minutes.

"They just never took the time out to learn to fly them properly," I said. "I heard the general report that there are no more complaints from the boys. I was hoping for a P-51 Mustang like you, Mei-lee, but then I'll fly anything. It's better than being on the ground any day."

"Oh, I love Mustang!" Mei-lee bragged, clasping her hands together excitedly.

"Lucky you," I said. "Let's get on our gear." I was starting to feel a little bit better since my loss. Staying busy was the key.

We were off to tame the Army's biggest Pursuits. "Tame" was quite a mild word to use, as many of the planes were in poor repair and stalling was still a constant event.

There wasn't much room inside the one-seat Pursuits. Cockpit space for baggage was nonexistent. I got out a small screwdriver and opened one of the two empty slots where ammunition would be stored later. I fit my underwear and shoes in one, unscrewed the other side and stuffed my uniform and toiletries in the other. I felt this was necessary, remembering one occasion when a restaurant refused to serve me dinner because I was wearing a flight suit instead of a skirt.

Before flying off to the East Coast, I took my custom-made wooden blocks with me to reach the rudder pedals.

The war was still in full throttle, with hundreds of planes to ferry. It was dead winter and no matter where I flew, it was foggy, pouring rain, or snowing, causing me painful sinus headaches and frostbitten fingers. The worst part was urinating into a bottle while flying 10,000 feet in the air. I kept saying my constant prayer, "Lord, surround and protect me. Fifinella, fly on my shoulder."

By now I had become valuable, because I could fly almost any type of aircraft, except for the bombers. I was truly serving my country. Our men were dying every day in the overseas battles, just like my Glenn had. These thoughts helped me cope better with my grief. Flying was exhilarating and it never failed to keep my mind off personal problems.

I made many plane deliveries and hopscotched all over the United States. The last delivery was to the Army base at New Castle, Delaware. I wearily took a bus to the closest hotel. Washing out my underwear and my Santiago Blues in the small sink, I hung them on the radiator to dry. I ironed my suit with a towel the best I could over the radiator, and then slept in the nude. I was too tired to go down and order the steak I'd been dreaming about. Closing my heavy lids, I smiled, remembering how friendly all the factory workers I'd met had been.

When I put on my uniform in the morning it looked forlornly wrinkled. *Darn*, I thought, *I keep forgetting to buy a toothbrush. I never thought I'd be away from base this long. Why didn't I learn how untrustworthy the Army was when they told me I would only be on a short trip?*

Thirty days, 17 states, 10 airplanes, 11,000 miles and one pathetic-looking uniform later, I finally boarded a commercial airline back to my base in Palm Springs. I recalled the meeting in the barracks before I left where we were told to inform the flight surgeon when we had our periods. How did the Army expect me to tell him when I was traveling? The whole topic was absurd.

I gazed out the window of the plane, thinking about all the weather I flew in—fog, rain, snow and sleet. There had been one or two close calls, but then there was always that possibility when it involved bad weather. A routine ferry trip could turn out to be a wild ride. Luckily, Fifinella had watched over me and I was glad to be heading toward sunny Palm Springs. Fatigue overcame me as I closed my bleary eyes. A soldier disturbed me and asked for a pillow.

"I'm not the stewardess," I said indignantly, sitting up taller.

"Then what are those wings for?" the private sheepishly asked, pointing at my uniform.

"I'm a ferry pilot for the Army Airforces," I said, staring him down.

"Huh? Oh, you mean you waitress on the planes and they let you wear the wings as a compliment?" He shrugged his shoulders.

"No, I ferry the planes, like I said." I grew more exasperated by the minute.

"You, you do?" he answered "All by yourself?"

"Yes," I said, averting my weary eyes to the side window.

"Well, who flies the plane?" He sounded truly confused.

"I do! Look, I'm not a senior Girl Scout, now leave me alone!"

In desperate need of some rest, I turned my head away from the dumb young man and pretended to nap. My once patient attitude had been lost along with my Glenn. Fatigue settled over me like a heavy blanket. The soldier eventually left with a dumbfounded look on his face, probably thinking a girl could never fly an airplane. I drifted off, remembering a few days back when I was delivering a Curtis P-40 Warhawk. That honey sure could fly fast!

Back at the base I ran into Myrna and Mei-lee having coffee in the mess hall.

"How's your ferrying going?" asked Myrna, who avoided eye contact by stirring her coffee.

"I'm beat. I just finished a 30-day run." I slouched onto the bench next to Mei-lee.

"That long time," Mei-lee said, nodding her head.

"You gals look pretty worn out yourselves," I yawned.

"You missed all the terrible news here at the base," Myrna said in a quiet voice as she nervously refashioned her dull-brown bun.

"What happened?" I sat up straighter.

"A P-51 crashed and burst into flames. Eleanor wasn't able to escape."

"Oh, my God, she was in my ammunitions class," I said.

"We were all pretty broken up about losing her. Betty

and Lenora quit on the spot they were so upset," Myrna said.

"You mean they quit the WASPs?" I said in disbelief.

"They home," Mei-lee added sadly.

"Do they know what went wrong?"

"The investigation concluded that the engine was not pre-tested at the factory. The steel in the valves was faulty." Myrna drummed her fingers on the mess hall table.

"I've been hearing of an awful lot of problems occurring because of careless production," I said.

"Like what?" asked Mei-lee, pushing her lunch aside.

"At one base, I heard a WASP lost a wing because some lazy factory worker filled in a hole with chewing gum rather than with a rivet."

"God!" Myrna said. "It's enough to make you want to quit." She looked at me briefly.

"I don't know what to believe anymore. On my 30-day ferry run, there was a lot of talk about traitors in the ranks of the mechanics," I said, gritting my teeth.

"What else?" asked Mei-lee.

"WASPs in all the different states were telling me mechanics have crossed fuel lines with coolant lines, that tires were expertly slashed not to blow on takeoff, but only on landing. One WASP at the Romulus Base in Michigan told me they all get their parachutes inspected before each flight, ever since a pilot found a small vial of acid with a loose stopper tucked in a fold!"

Myrna seemed discomfited by this line of conversation and abruptly changed the subject. "I was off delivering a P-38 Lockheed Lightning to Indiana and radioed the tower requesting landing instructions. The tower boy answered, 'I have a P-38 in sight. Where are you?' I impatiently rocked my wings back and forth, yelling into my radio, 'Can't you see my wings?' He answered, 'Just follow the P-38.' Infuriated, I screamed, 'I *am* the P-38!' 'Oh my gosh,' he shouted, 'Are you a girl?'"

Mei-lee burst out laughing. I snickered, relieved to be off the topic of poor Eleanor's terrible fate. We had to prove ourselves repeatedly, even though we knew that the WASPs had a lower percentage of crashes than all the male cadet pilots. Accidents and deaths were all part of the life of a test pilot. I tried not to think about it, but how could I accept all the death that kept flying at me? First May, then my honey, now Eleanor. I knew we could quit anytime, since we were not part of the military. I reflected on when May had died and Lana said to me, "We do not have time to mourn, there is far too much work to do!" I certainly didn't agree with her at the time, but she was right on the beam. I sure missed her and hoped she ended up in Palm Springs. I could use my true friend to console me at this point in my life.

Chapter Sixteen: The Night Witches

At mail call I got a letter from Lana and eagerly tore it open.

Dear Violet:

I wish I could find something comforting to say to you about the loss of your fiancé. Believe it or not, the only feeling that comes to mind for me is "time heals all wounds." This may sound annoying and probably reminds you of our silly Adele, but it really has been a saying that has rung true for me. Prayer can also help. Keep praying for God to protect and surround you, as you always have, and don't give up. It can be a great comfort as well as hope. Now for some news to keep your mind off your troubles.

As you can see from the postmark, I am no longer towing targets. I'm in Dayton, Ohio, flying high-altitude missions. I was instructed to fly to 15,000 feet, come back, and then undergo a physical examination. After entering the classroom, I was told to write my name on the chalkboard. Get this; I drew the letter L, and then fell over! Since then, the Army has decided it's dangerous not to use oxygen above 10,000 feet!

On the next test flight, I made the mistake of drinking

a cup of coffee, which of course made me need to pee. My stomach throbbed and cramped. I squirmed in my heavy fleece-lined flight suit and bounced around on my bulky seat pack parachute, trying to fight Mother Nature. As I wiggled back and forth, Frank, my co-pilot, shot me a look, and smirked, saying, "Here, try the relief tube." I scolded him saying, "Very funny. You know as well as I do that women's plumbing is not the same as men's." Well, of course he knew that the small funnel attached to the hose was totally useless for the female anatomy. Then he says, "Here, take the portable oxygen supply, it'll last you only two minutes, so don't dawdle." I struggled to the back of the plane with my parachute banging against my legs. I had one hand on the oxygen mask and with the other hand, I somehow managed to unbutton the back flap of my flight suit. I quickly relieved myself into the open two-target hatch at 30,000 feet altitude, in a temperature of minus 20 degrees. I made it back to the cockpit gasping for breath while the male crew enjoyed a hearty laugh.

Speaking of oxygen, I have found the best way to recover from a hangover is to take a big whiff. You should try it sometime!

Oh, by the way, I'm now an official member of the "Mile-High Club." My newest beau (Bill) and I made love at 5,000 feet in the back of a B-26 while our buddy, Joe, was piloting!

I'm sure you are wondering why my handwriting is shaky. Don't you ever tell anyone, but guess where I'm writing this? From behind the wheel! The weather is calm and all I have to do is trim the ship, then it flies straight and level by itself. I have one hand on the wheel and my feet on the rudders and look around every few minutes. Sounds like awfully hard work, doesn't it? I'm right "on the beam," and don't have to worry about navigating. Don't fret; I won't make a practice of writing while I'm flying!

Remember kid, keep a stiff upper lip and keep on flyin' Fifinella!

Have a Merry Christmas!

Love always, Lana

P.S. I got accepted to Pursuit School. Hope to see you soon, my dear friend.

I surprised myself by laughing out loud. I missed my crazy friend Lana. I looked around to see if anyone had heard, never thinking I could laugh again after losing my Glenn. Maybe Lana was right about that old saying, after all. While my mood was in an upswing, I sat down to write to Mother and Dad.

Dear Mother and Dad:

I know my ferrying is more important than thinking about Glenn. I am glad to be occupied, serving an important purpose in life, but I still grieve for him with all my heart.

I have been flying to almost every state. After the funeral, I flew into New York over Niagara Falls, landed in Buffalo, and took a bus to New York City to see the Rockettes. It was amazing to watch their beautiful legs kick up to eye level. I was really mesmerized by their sparkling costumes and synchronized dancing.

It's Christmas Eve and I miss all of you badly. I went to Midnight Mass and a few familiar hymns cheered me right up.

Read this letter to the boys for me and please have them send me more of their drawings of bombers. The one you sent that Tommy drew of the P-40 is very darling.

Merry Christmas to all,

Love, Violet

A few days later, as I headed toward the barracks, I ran into Mei-lee.

"You look tired, Violet," she said.

"Yes, I had quite a rough flight today. Were you able to pick up any letters for me at mail call?"

"You got letter, here." She reached into the pocket of her coveralls.

"Thanks," I said, looking at the return address on the envelope she held out. I eagerly tore open Lana's letter.

Camp Davis, North Carolina

Dear Vi:

Your last letter seemed a little cheerier and gave me hope that you will survive your loss. Sometimes God does have a purpose in mind, even though it does not seem remotely possible that something good can come from bad!

Here's my latest adventure to bring you a well-needed laugh.

I saved my ration coupons and paycheck and went into town and picked up the cutest ensemble to wear to the Officers' Club dance. I wore a cadet-blue whirl skirt and crepe blouse with a very revealing neckline. My cunning blue kid patent leather pumps had jaunty bows with open toes and 2 ½-inch heels. Let me tell you, I was decked out to the nines! A sharp-looking lieutenant named William gave me the onceover and asked me to dance. I let him do all the talking and boy

197

could he jabber! William starts bragging to me about going off to war, "flying a P-47 with a huge engine." He then snuggled up real close during the slow dance, whispering, "You never know, it could quit after takeoff!" I simply held him tighter, flirtatiously saying, "Oh, William, I hope you'll be all right."

The next morning I went into operations with my flight suit on and there he was. You should have seen his double take. He had no idea I was a test pilot!

"You never let on last night that you were a pilot," he says with an accusing voice.

"Yep, I'm a test pilot," I tell him nonchalantly.

Then he says to me, trying to save face, "I'd rather be in combat risking my life than just testing airplanes in the States."

So I say to him, "William, I loved dancing with you last night, but can't you get it through your thick head that someone's got to test the planes in order for you to safely fly them into combat?"

He counters me with, "I think you WASPs just like the thrill of flying a different plane every day."

"It's not as glamorous as you think. I have to get up in the cold dark just to get to the flight line by daylight. My flight suit is heavy and cumbersome, especially with my 30-pound parachute on. I'm always feeling either hot or cold, most of the planes don't even have a heater and some don't have radios if I have to call for help. Before boarding any ship, I read the write-ups, which can be damn frightening. Some have

statements like 'smelled funny' or 'gas gauge not reading properly.' After takeoff, I have to hope that the mechanics did their jobs and really fixed the problems like the papers said they did. It's up to the WASPs to be sure the airplanes were satisfactorily repaired by testing them."

"Gosh, Lana," he says, "I guess I see your point."

I say, "It's like this, William. I am as proud as you are to fly for my country. You may fly 'em into battle, but I'm the one getting them ready for you."

If only you could have seen his face! I got more respect from him after that. William sure was a swell dancer, even if he was a braggart and the Officers' Club is the only relaxing time I ever get.

Well, kid, thought I'd share this little gem with you to brighten your day. I feel like a sister to you and hope your heart will mend soon.

Love, Lana

P.S. I leave tomorrow for Palm Springs. I hope you will be around.

I placed the letter under my pillow and got ready for bed, happy my friend would be by my side once again.

Lana successfully completed her four weeks of training and we went on assignment together along with Myrna, Adele, and Mei-lee. Our job was to move airplanes, and move 'em we did.

The P-39 Airacobras at the Niagara Falls Factory had red stars painted on them for the Russians, and the five of us got the privilege of delivering them to Great Falls, Montana for the government Lend-Lease program.

I felt a bit anxious as I landed on a fresh, snow-cleared runway strip. I was still inexperienced when it came to handling Pursuits in winter weather, and was thankful the landing was smooth.

I had on my woolen underwear and a ski sweater, topped off with a lined lamb's wool leather flight jacket. All these clothes, including a leather facemask under the helmet, should have kept me warm in the 10-degree cold, but I still felt chilled. Sometimes the heater worked, but this wasn't one of those times. The leather jacket got so stiff it was hard to turn around and get out of the Pursuit. The 30-pound parachute pack only added to the cumbersome maneuver. I could hardly believe that just the day before I was sunbathing in Palm Springs.

I was the first to arrive, and took advantage of the solitude. I trudged through the snow, taking in the panoramic view of the mountains as I sucked in the fresh, crisp air. I felt glorious now that I was freed from the cramped cockpit. The view on land was as magnificent as it had been in the sky. Reluctantly, I hiked back toward the hangar, picking my legs up high in the thick, deep snow.

The mechanic grinned at me as I took off my chamois facemask. "You look like Lon Chaney in *The Phantom of the Opera*," he said. His horrid breath reeked of whiskey.

I had heard this joke before, but I gave him a false little laugh, knowing from past experience that it was wise to get real friendly with the mechanics, since they were a key part in my safety.

"Name's Donald," he said, running his eyes all over my body—an act I found very annoying.

"Nice to meet you, Donald. I'm Violet from the Palm Springs base," I said politely, though I wanted to tell him to stop staring at me. I moved back a bit to give myself some space from his alcoholic breath.

"What brings you to the icy state of Montana, gal?" He rubbed a three-day stubble on his chin, giving me the onceover again.

"I'm delivering this P-39 for the Russian Lend-Lease program."

"I met some of those Russian women pilots when I was in Alaska working on some of the planes. They're called 'Night Witches' because they fly missions at night," Donald bragged.

"You don't say?" Now he had my attention.

"I'll be goddamned, here comes one of their planes now. The Russians must be desperate to allow dames to do men's work."

"I wonder if the Army will ever use the WASPs for combat," I said.

"I don't think gals will ever be used in the service as long as men are around to do the job right," Donald answered, purposely pushing out his chest.

I snorted with disgust. "I've got to get my papers signed off," I said, grateful for a reason to get away from this bigheaded man.

I trampled through the snow toward the Russian's plane, which, much to my surprise, was a biplane just like the Jenny.

Two Soviet women pilots climbed down from their aircraft. I reached out my hand to the first one. "Hi, I'm Violet Willey. I'm here delivering a Pursuit for the Lend-Lease program."

"Lieutenant Lydia Levacoff. My co-pilot, Sonya Bersova, 588th Night Bomber Regiment. Thank you for your services," she said in a thick Russian accent.

We shook hands as I looked at their plane. "What type of airplane are you flying?"

"Come," the lieutenant said as she gestured me toward her plane. "This is a Po-2. It was designed in 1927 and the beauty of the plane is that it is capable of descending on any landscape."

"It reminds me of the first airplane I flew in as a young girl," I said nostalgically.

"How so?" the lieutenant asked.

"It's made of fabric and wood," I said, feeling the wing affectionately.

"Yes, that's her downfall. It is a fire hazard in combat and the fuel tanks are not shielded, so it is very vulnerable to being set on fire if hit. At least it can carry two 1,200 pound bombs and it does have a machine gun in the rear cockpit," Lydia said proudly.

With my gloved hand I felt one of the white roses painted on the side of the Po-2. I smiled, glancing at the pilots.

Lieutenant Levacoff looked pleased that I had noticed them. "Those are for my hits. I am called, 'The White Rose of Stalingrad,'" she said.

"Hits?" I asked, surprised.

She put her hands on her hips. "Each of these roses signifies my successes in bombing the Nazis."

"Oh," I said meekly. "Women aren't allowed to serve in combat here in America, but I know now, despite what all the men say, women can obviously be quite an asset to this war."

A gust of wind came off the snow-capped mountains, causing me to shiver. I noticed it did not faze these tough, young Soviet women. I had heard it could get down to 40 below where they came from.

The lieutenant walked over to the Pursuit I had flown in for her and touched the red star painted on the side, then smiled. I beamed back, knowing that the factory workers had also painted a tiny purple violet on the other side just for me.

"Would you care to join me for a hot cup of coffee before your trip?" I invited.

"We would be quite honored, thank you," the lieutenant answered. Her co-pilot, Sonya, who was taller than her superior, never said a word. She just watched and listened to our conversation. I thought she either did not know any English, or was following a military order to only allow her commander to speak.

They followed my lead across the slushy snow. I couldn't help but notice how big and clumsy their knee-high, fur-lined leather boots were.

We walked by Donald. He waved. I could tell by his face he wanted to meet the Soviets, but I certainly wasn't interested in hearing his negative banter about women in combat again. I just glanced at him and led the ladies on past. I was looking forward to learning all about the Night Witches.

Chapter Seventeen: An Adventure for Lana

After filling our cups with coffee, we sat at a long, narrow table in the mess hall. Lieutenant Lydia Levacoff took off her leather helmet. Under it was a furry cap with floppy dog ears down to her shoulders.

Very clever, I thought. *I'm sure it helps with the cold where these gals fly.*

Then officer Sonya Bersova took off her helmet, revealing a bright white, close-fitting silk cap with the same type of ear pads. She noticed me looking at it and broke her silence. "My cap, made of parachute silk, keep me warm."

"How practical," I said. Her English was certainly not as clear as her superior's.

The lieutenant took off her oversized, high-collared tunic coat with large, red, stiff shoulder boards. Around her neck was a multicolored scarf.

I touched it. "How beautiful," I said.

"It is also made of parachute silk."

"The colors are gorgeous."

"It is dyed from herbs and berries."

Their baggy khaki blouses and loose trousers were obviously large men's uniforms, reminding me of the zoot suit that was first issued to me in basic training.

After a few sips of hot coffee, the lieutenant removed her furry hat, pointed to her hair, and said, "This is my mop. When I first enlisted, I had beautiful, long, brown curly hair, but we were required to cut it off. I got peroxide from a nearby hospital and bleached it white to at least give it some kind of style. We are not allowed to have long hair like you," she said, pointing to one of my braids.

I had never seen such shocking hair like that, and quickly changed the subject in order not to comment about it. "Tell me, I've heard you're called 'Night Witches' and fly missions at night. How do you do this?"

"It is the Nazis who call us *Nachthexen*—Night Witches. Our male pilot comrades call us 'Little Sisters.' Our flying begins at sunset and ends at dawn. We use the dark of night for protection. Our Po-2s have a noise muffler to approach targets undetected. First, we send a noisy plane with the engine powered up, like one of your Pursuits, to attract the attention of the German ground defense. Then the Po-2 silently follows and drops the bombs. One night, we raided the Germans 18 times. The psychological impact of the night-long harassment is almost too much for the Germans to endure."

Fascinated, my eyes got bigger and bigger with every sentence the lieutenant uttered. "What amazing bravery you display. It almost puts my work to shame."

Lieutenant Levacoff continued, "This is something we must do, then the Germans never get any peace at night. Ever since they shot down and killed my lover, Illya, I will continue to defend my Motherland. Every attack, every bombing, is a dance with death!"

I immediately thought of Glenn. I was astonished at how much Lieutenant Levacoff and I had in common.

Officer Bersova sneezed and pulled out the most beautiful handkerchief I had ever seen. The edges were covered with all sorts of colorful, tiny flowers.

"What an exquisite handkerchief you have there."

"Oh, we embroider all time; it settles nerves."

"How did you learn to fly airplanes?" I asked Lieutenant Levacoff.

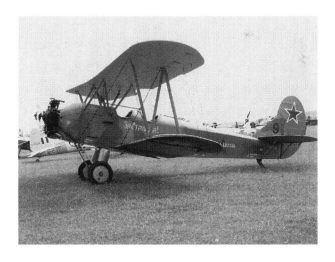

"When I was 17, I entered one of the civil pilot schools, where I obtained my license. We were taught in a few months what it takes most people years to learn. I signed up after reading an announcement stating that the women selected would have to be frontline combat pilots, just like men. After I enlisted, the Nazis captured over 400,000 prisoners. We still have a lot of work to do. Now, tell me about yourself," she said with a friendly smile, as she smoothed down her white, boyish-cropped hair.

I told her about my experience, and how we were only allowed to ferry the planes from the factories to the bases, but never in combat.

"What's your gun for?" she asked, noticing my Colt .45 pistol.

"Oh, it's to guard our airplanes. In case anyone tries to steal them, we're trained to shoot the fuel tank."

"We carry pistols to defend ourselves," Lieutenant Levacoff said, displaying her gun to me. She downed her last sip of coffee, then stood up. "We must be off now, we have a long journey ahead. On behalf of our country, we wish to thank you for supplying us aircraft. It certainly aids in our severe shortage." She buckled her extra large belt on her uniform coat and pulled it tight.

"Good luck, and may God be with you," I said with great admiration.

"Good luck to you too, comrade. Everyone thinks we face death openly, bravely, but it is not true. We are just as afraid as our men, and just as patriotic, as I know you are. We both offer our skills as pilots in the defense of our countries."

I followed them outside into the brisk air and watched the lieutenant fly off in the P-39. Officer Bersova took off in the Po-2 shortly thereafter. As I watched, it occurred to me that the Night Witches didn't wear parachutes. I whispered a prayer for their safety.

Just as I was about to go back to the base to get warm, I saw a Pursuit fly in. There was Lana, stiffly getting out. I tramped through the snow as fast as I could. "Hi, how was your flight? My P-39 was a dream, except for the faulty heater. How was yours?" My words made cold puffs in the air.

"It was fairly smooth, but this snowy weather makes it a bit tricky to handle." She reached into her pocket, grabbed a cigarette, and lit it.

"Let's go to the mess hall and get warm. I've got quite a story to tell you." I affectionately put my arm around her waist as we clomped together through the deep Montana snow.

I gave Donald a small wave as we walked past him. I could tell he wanted me to introduce Lana, but I didn't want to engage in further conversation with this obnoxious man.

Once in the mess hall with Lana, I enthusiastically told her all about meeting the Soviet pilots.

"I'm astonished by how much Lieutenant Levacoff and I had in common. The Po-2 was just like the Jenny I used to fly. Also, we both took civil pilot classes and lost our men in the war." I looked down toward the mess hall floor.

"It must've been quite an honor to meet a real Soviet Night Witch," Lana said as she stubbed out her cigarette. She reached over and patted my hand, sensing my sadness. "I can't wait for tonight when Adele and Mei-lee get in; we'll have a great bash in the hotel room!"

"I'm looking forward to some R and R, myself," I said. "Whenever I think of all us ole bay mates being together again, I can't help thinking about May." I rose and zipped up my jacket, trying to resist feeling depressed.

That night the five of us gathered in our Montana hotel room. The drinks flowed freely. The party was off to a good start as we whooped it up and swapped stories.

"Remember the Christmas Eve party we had in the mess hall at Avenger?" I said with a giggle, feeling the effects of my Tom Collins.

"I'll never forget Lana's striptease act!" Adele exploded, adding, "Laughter's the best medicine!"

"Remember when I started out the show in my Santiago Blues and the asinine turban we used to wear, then I stripped that off, revealing the ole zoot suit?" Lana said, parading around the room.

"You must've been the only one that didn't burn your turban in the bonfire when the Army said we didn't have to wear them anymore." I smiled broadly.

"I had a feeling that jackass hat would come in handy for a joke later on," Lana snickered as she took a swig from a bottle.

"I was hooting and hollering all over the place when you stripped off the coveralls and I watched you prancing around in your bright-red long johns!" I yelled loudly, and caught a bad case of hiccups.

"Violet, you drunk!" Mei-Lee said playfully, sloshing down her second whiskey sour.

"Remember when the locusts swarmed down on the base? They were all over our lockers and beds. They even got in my eyes," Myrna said in her subdued voice.

"How could we forget that?" Adele said. "They even got in our food. The buzzing and humming drove me crazy. We had to be grounded because of the buggers getting into the engines. After it was all over, it took two days to clean them out of the barracks. Those locusts made me as nervous as a long-tailed cat in a room full of rocking chairs!" Adele threw her hands up in a high-spirited way.

"Remember when I was in the outhouse on the base and that damn Texas wind knocked it over and I was caught with my pants down?" I said, laughing so hard I fell off the bed onto the floor.

After much merriment, followed by yawning, we knew we shouldn't drink anymore. We did have to be in shape to fly back to Palm Springs. We went to our beds for some shut-eye. I rolled onto my back, then on my side, and rubbed my temples. I hoped the pulsating would stop so I could go off to slumberland and awaken refreshed for the journey back to the base.

Lana was the first one up and into the shower. She came out with a towel wrapped around her slender body and another one fashioned around her head. She stomped over to my bed and gave me a poke. "Get up, sleepyhead. We've got a long flight back to Palm Springs."

"Ooh," I groaned, rolling over and rubbing my forehead. "My head is killing me."

"Nothing a good strong cup of Joe won't cure," she said, toweling her hair dry.

I managed to swing my legs over the side of the bed and sat up, feeling a little dizzy.

"Violet, did I tell you about the blond hunk I met at the Officers' Club in Palm Springs?" Lana asked as she pinned up her wet hair.

"Nooo," I said, not feeling well enough or awake enough to listen to another story about Lana's many boyfriends.

"Well," she continued, ignoring my indifference, "Bill is almost 6'1", and a lieutenant. He's flown more bombers overseas than he can count and he thinks I'm a real pipperoo!" She sat on my bed, looked into her compact, and applied her luscious lipstick.

"I'm happy for you, Lana, but get off my bed. I'd better hit the shower before the others wake up." I tried getting up, but Lana wouldn't budge.

"Violet, he's meeting me at the tarmac when I arrive, and I was wondering if I could possibly borrow your pearl necklace again? I think he might be the one!" Lana squeezed my arm, a pleading look in her eyes.

"All right, Lana, you can borrow it, but get off. I need to get rid of this hangover in the shower." Impatient, I pushed her and went into the bathroom just in time, as I heard Mei-lee and Adele stirring.

At the flight line I checked and double-checked my fighter plane before taking off, thinking of how one of the WASPs had senselessly died in an AT-6 from a factory mechanical failure. We all knew she could have escaped if only the cockpit's roof latch had worked right. She must not have looked at the repair records, where it was noted that the latch had needed fixing. I knew she could have easily examined it before takeoff.

We were lined up nose-to-tail on the ramp. I was impatient to be on my way. Lana was first in line. The sound of her engine was sputtering and rough. This damn cold weather! I reassured myself that we had all done a thorough check, plus most of the boys seemed like competent mechanics. My Curtiss P-40 was a beauty—a sleek monoplane with a powerful, single-piston engine. I was looking forward to the liftoff. I massaged my temples, trying to soothe my headache.

Lana's Pursuit swiftly gained speed as it went down the runway. Her engine revved and backfired. I instantly thought this was a sure sign of trouble. The rear wheel lifted, and the tail was level with the nose as it rose upward. In a matter of seconds, the engine exhaust was glowing red-hot. Lana's plane settled toward the ground. It crashed as the landing gear collapsed, sending it scraping on its belly. The engine caught fire. The flames quickly spread to the fuel tank. I screamed, helplessly sitting in my plane, afraid to get out.

Smoke poured from the engine and sirens wailed. A fire truck and ambulance raced to Lana's P-40. My eyes widened and my body began to shake when I saw asbestos-clad men pull Lana out from the burning wreckage. Her flight suit was smoldering as she was lifted onto the stretcher.

I sat in my cockpit, dumbfounded, looking at all the smoke, and watched as the ambulance took off.

Control tower blared in my radio, "All planes return to the flight line immediately."

Myrna, Adele, Mei-lee and I all taxied back to where Lieutenant Fitch stood with his hands on his hips.

One by one we all got out as the lieutenant barked, "All flights have been canceled. Go back to your hotel room."

"What...what about Lana?" I asked, frozen to the spot.

"Director Cochran will be in charge of her body."

"Her *body*?"

Lieutenant Fitch ignored me. "Now ladies, you are dismissed. Your director has been notified and will arrive as soon as possible."

He looked directly at us, and did not move until we all walked slowly off the flight line.

Chapter Eighteen: The Sabotage

Adele made a coughing, choking noise as her eyes welled up with tears. Mei-lee outright sobbed, and Myrna held her. The four of us all cried together as we walked the half mile to our hotel room with our arms linked together.

Once inside, we crawled onto our separate beds, where a numbing silence took the place of our sobbing noises.

I was the first to speak. "Adele, let's go over to the hangar and talk to the mechanics—I want to know what happened to Lana's plane," I said, jabbing her bed.

"I was thinking the same thing. Let's go before Director Cochran gets here," Adele answered, wiping her swollen eyes with the back of her hand.

Jacob slid out from under the P-40. "Unbelievable," he said, scratching his head.

"What did you find?" I asked, glad I had arrived at the right time to find some answers.

"There was definitely sugar in the fuel tank." He stood up, wiping his greasy hands on his coveralls.

"My God, that's outright sabotage! What's the reason for this? We aren't the enemy!" Adele screamed at him.

"I don't know how to answer that question. All I know is that as a mechanic, I've seen plenty of monkey business ever since the war started." Jacob continued inspecting the plane as he talked.

"What type of monkey business?" I asked, looking suspiciously around for that obnoxious mechanic, Donald.

"Well, one time a crashed plane came into the hangar and after several of us inspected it, we found handfuls of grass in the fuel tank," Jacob said, fingering each rivet on Lana's P-40.

"That's about as stupid as a screen door on a submarine," Adele said.

"Why in God's name would one of our own men do such a thing?" I asked, my lips pursed tightly.

"That's a hard question to answer, but several of my mechanic buddies and I figure it must have been some mean soldier who was sick of working overtime. I've also overheard some mechanics saying that the WASPs are just a bunch of rich women taking the safe jobs, forcing men into the line of fire." Jacob searched inside the plane and pulled out something charred.

"God save us!" I shrieked.

Jacob held a string of blackened pearls in his hand. I grabbed them and walked out of the hangar before Jacob and Adele could say a word.

Late the next morning, the director arrived, knocked on our hotel room door, then entered.

"What happened to Lana's P-40?" I demanded, clenching and unclenching my fists.

"We know that there was some goddamned mischief that caused that accident!" Adele ranted, twisting her unruly hair.

"Now girls, try to calm down," Director Cochran said, straightening her chic pleated skirt. She stared straight ahead as she spoke to us all in a rehearsed manner. "I have been informed that what happened to Lana was a mechanical failure. The Bell Factory has sent out several representatives to the base to confirm this."

"Director Cochran, this was outright sabotage! Why, it's premeditated murder! We did our own investigating last night, and one of the mechanics said there was sugar in her fuel tank!" I shouted, my face turning redder by the minute.

"You know that the mechanics are overworked," the director sternly stated.

"Mechanical failure, what bullshit," I said, surprising myself by cursing.

Mei-lee sobbed as she said, "How we know it won't happen again?"

Ignoring Mei-lee, Director Cochran continued with her canned talk. "As you all know, there is a severe shortage of men. The Army still needs you girls. Let's show them what you're still made of and ferry the planes to win this war!"

"Director, we're still not even part of the Army. Tell me, what benefits will poor Lana's family get from this senseless death?" Adele said. "I guess God only helps those who help themselves."

Myrna never said a word. She just sat on her bed with her fingers firmly interlocked on her lap.

Director Cochran simply walked toward the door, her shiny, black pumps clicking. Before she turned the knob, Mei-lee shouted, "I quit!"

Cochran ignored her and abruptly left.

"Mechanical failure, what bullshit," I said again, my voice quivering. I realized that this was one of Lana's expressions, which brought tears to my eyes. I glanced over at Myrna. Her silence was aggravating me even more.

"I still can't believe that there was really sugar in the tank!" Adele said, stomping around the floor in a circle.

"I can't take death. We not even in combat," said Mei-lee, teary-eyed. "I just want to go home, to my people." She sniffled.

"All I can think about is the sight of Lana's plane burning up," Adele said in a subdued voice, while folding up her belongings.

"Who will go with me to transport Lana's body to her parents?" I asked, raising my voice impatiently.

"I go with you, but after that I go home," Mei-lee volunteered.

Adele said, "Hell hath no fury like a woman scorned."

"One more item that needs to be taken care of," I said.

"What more can there possibly be?" Adele hollered, tapping her foot.

"First, we all need to chip in and buy a casket. Does anyone have any extra money?" I asked.

"I some. I gladly give it for Lana," Mei-lee said in a subdued tone.

"I might be able to get some money from my parents," Adele said, refolding her clothes over and over again.

Myrna spoke for the first time. "I have some savings from my husband's death benefit."

Death benefits. It was dreadful that Lana's family would get nothing. Myrna received $10,000 after her husband died, just as Glenn's parents did.

"I can cash in my war bonds," I said, feeling more depressed by the minute.

"Well, that's settled. Let's try and get some sleep. We'll have to get up early to pick out a casket," Adele said.

I was numb going through the motions about the business of my best friend's death. I didn't want to let myself feel the full reality of missing her.

Early the next morning, we went into town and had a pine box delivered to the base. We noticed two plain-clothes investigators on site to watch the refueling of the Pursuits to deter any further acts of sabotage or tampering.

I threw my belongings in a duffle bag and headed to the main office with Mei-lee to receive permission for a leave of absence. It was a good thing that it would take two long train rides to get from Great Falls to New York. My hot temper needed the time to cool down. If we were in the Army Airforces, we could have taken a plane to Lana's parents' house.

A diminutive undertaker met us at the station with the death certificate. "Don't forget, you must purchase a ticket for the coffin," he said, and walked away before we could even balk at the idea.

Mei-lee and I were on the train to Bronx, New York, to take Lana home. We took turns guarding her casket, even though chances were slim that someone would steal a dead body.

Still in shock, I was not looking forward to seeing Lana's parents. All I knew about her family was that she was the oldest of four girls and that her dad had been against her joining the WASPs.

My innocence was now gone. I thought it had vanished after Glenn died, but now sabotage was all I could think about.

Several days later, we arrived in New York. I found this city to be a most confusing place. There were many cars honking, and traffic lights at every corner. Interspersed between the cars and trucks were policemen on horses. I was glad I had explored it once before, when I saw the Rockettes at Radio City Music Hall. At least I'd learned how to hail a taxicab if we needed one. A funeral director met us at the station and was kind enough to drive us to Lana's family's apartment house in his hearse.

Mei-lee was wide-eyed the whole trip as she watched the city pass by us like a movie through the cab window. She shook my leg and pointed. "The buildings are tall, tall walls!"

"It's an astonishing place. I've only been here once before, after a flight into Niagara Falls, and it still amazes me."

"I never see anything like this," Mei-lee said as she stared, transfixed, out the window.

"You get used to it after you live here awhile," the funeral director said with a big smile on his face. "Here we are, Fordham Avenue, ladies."

"Look," Mei-lee said, pointing at the entrance to the Walton's apartment house.

Dusty, weathered bronze lions flanked the front doors. I nodded, looking upward, and saw in a window a child's drawing of a gold star. I thought that must be Lana's apartment and one of her sisters must have drawn it. The Army naturally didn't allow an official star posted in honor of Lana's death, because of the nonmilitary status of the WASPs. This made my anger flare once more. We climbed the long cement steps, forlornly passing the lions, and opened the weathered, brown double doors.

"We'll probably have to take an elevator," I said to Mei-lee, looking at a scrap of paper that read *702.*

"I never in elevator," Mei-lee said eagerly.

After pushing the elevator button over and over, then watching to see if the numbers of the floors changed, I let out an exhausted sigh. "Let's find the stairs."

We walked toward the staircase, which spiraled upwards. Higher and higher we climbed, until at last we saw a big number seven painted on the wall and pulled open the heavy door. Number 702 was the first door down the hall. I quietly knocked on it, not knowing what to expect, and positioned my beret on my head while Mei-lee smoothed her skirt.

Mrs. Walton opened the door. "Please come in, girls. We've been expecting you."

We followed Mrs. Walton into the dark, cluttered living room. Lana's little sisters were on the floor playing with paper dolls—an Army nurse, a Red Cross worker, and a third paper doll, which was a Marine fighter.

On a small wooden table were piles of telegrams. I discreetly picked one up while Mrs. Walton went to get her husband. It read: *She was a wonderful person. If it is any comfort, she died where she was most content, in the air. I will never forget her. My deepest sympathies, Rosemary Wright.*

I was amazed to see Rosemary's name. How thoughtful of her to send a note, even though she had washed out of the WASPs and was now at home. She must have read the newspaper article about Lana's demise.

I moved a Little Orphan Annie coloring book on the couch aside and Mei-lee sat beside me.

" 'Dorable paper dolls," Mei-lee said to Lana's sisters.

The oldest one answered shyly, "Thank you."

Mr. Walton came into the room, sneering. My hands were trembling after meeting Lana's mother, and now they were outright shaking. I clenched them firmly together on my lap.

Without any greeting whatsoever, Mr. Walton said, "None of you girls had any business getting involved in this war. It's men's work." His large brown eyes stared at us accusingly. "It's not my fault I didn't have any boys."

"Uh, uh, yes sir." I looked down at the girls silently dressing their paper dolls. "Your daughter was my best friend in the WASPs, sir, and I'm so sorry. All the bay mates chipped in to pay for her funeral." I spoke rapidly, hoping to ease the tension.

Mrs. Walton came in and whisked Lana's sisters into the kitchen.

Mr. Walton raised his finger, pointing at us, saying, "Your people killed our daughter, now you can bury her! I never gave her permission to go into this war!"

I mustered as much courage as I could, got up, and turned to face him. "The funeral will be the day after tomorrow, at one o'clock at your church. We'll be at Hotel Matheson if you need us."

Mr. Walton glared. "Crazy women pilots," He buried his face in his hands, muffling a deep, sobbing noise. He took out his handkerchief, blew his nose, and left the room.

Mei-lee looked at me with a frightened, questioning face as she rose from the couch. I took her hand and we walked out of the apartment. I burst into tears, unable to keep myself together any longer. Mei-lee also broke down as she embraced me.

I clutched her, relieved that I was not alone to deal with this messy situation, which seemed to spell out, "Thanks a lot, here's your daughter, without benefits, recognition, or honor."

The day of the funeral, General Arnold and Director Cochran stood outside the church. They nodded at Mei-lee and me as we got out of the cab. We were surprised to see Lana's casket draped with the American flag. The general had obviously made an exception to allow this military procedure.

I was consoled when I saw the Walton family coming up the street, all dressed in black. Thank God Mr. Walton had changed his mind and had come.

The general was the first to speak. "Kindly accept my condolences on your daughter's accident. She was an asset to our country."

Mr. Walton gave the general a nasty look. "That's not our daughter in that coffin! Open it!" he commanded, pointing his finger at the coffin.

"I'm sorry, Mr. Walton, regulations forbid opening a sealed coffin," the general said quietly.

"Open it!" he shouted again.

General Arnold glanced at the director, then removed the flag and handed it to her.

Mr. Walton opened the coffin a few inches and peered inside. He shut it quickly. "She's dead, all right. You and your organization killed her. Come Edith, let's go inside."

Mrs. Walton put her arms around her three girls and followed her husband into the church.

During Mass, I glanced around and was pleased to see there was standing room only. Mei-lee and I sat in the second pew with the Walton family.

After the long Mass, we slowly filed outside. I looked down the aisle and spotted Rosemary holding her bible. She must have come all the way from Indiana. There were quite a few WASPs there, but of course, not everyone could make it because of their flying duties. Huge bouquets of flowers filled the altar, making the statue of Mother Mary barely visible. Lana's short existence had touched many lives.

The only way I could keep my sorrowful emotions inside was by picturing the obscene sabotage of Lana's plane, which made me feel furious, instead.

After Mass, Adele and I made our way toward the crowded church hall for the eulogy.

Director Cochran began the eulogy. "As it can happen in any war, Lana Walton gave her life. Let us pause to remember all of our sister pilots who died before us in the sky."

Pastor Monaghan then said, "Let us weep as we open our hearts for the family Lana leaves behind."

General Arnold added, "Let us pray that our planes will be infallible and our engines never fail us. The Army will long remember Lana's service and final sacrifice. Do not be afraid. Lana Walton is now in that special place in Heaven that God has reserved for His pilots."

Mei-lee made short breathing noises, trying hard to suppress her tears.

I stood up, fidgeted with the buttons on my uniform jacket, and walked up to the podium.

"Lana was a true friend. She helped me strive to do my best. The Army has lost a valuable asset and I am very sad that she has left us." Overcome with grief, I couldn't finish what I had prepared to say. I went back to the pew, burying my sobs in my hands. I dried my eyes with Mei-lee's hanky and glanced over at Lana's three little sisters, who sat huddled together. The oldest one kept blowing her nose and dabbing her eyes, while the younger two looked bewildered and confused.

What a senseless death, I thought. Angrily, I took the charred pearls out of my skirt pocket and squeezed them so tight that the beads left round impressions as they ground into my palm.

Chapter Nineteen: Back at Home

I was quite worn out when I arrived back at Palm Springs. I went into the barracks to lie on my cot and found a letter on it. The postmark was from Washington, D.C. I threw my beret off and sat down to read it.

```
To All Women Airforce Service Pilots:

We sincerely appreciate your service in the war
effort. We will never again look at women as a
flying experiment as your losses were much lower
all the male cadet trainees. It is time for women
to step down and let our men take over. I am sorry
to inform you that the Women Airforce Service
program will be deactivated on 12/20/44.

Happy Landings, Always,

General Henry H. Arnold

Director Jacqueline Cochran
```

I reread the letter in disbelief. Yes, the war was winding down. In June, Allied bombers had successfully hit the Germans, but the war was not entirely over.

Since February, there were more and more American male pilots streaming back to the bases than ever before. I had been hoping the letter was my acceptance into

Bomber School. I had been looking forward to flying the B-29 Super Fortress. This bomber was three stories tall and cost the Army Airforces three billion dollars to build.

Depression engulfed me once more. I was devastated. Flying was the only event that kept my mind away from all my troubles. I looked over at Mei-lee's cot and it was bare. She really had quit. I didn't have any friends here any longer. Adele irritated me too much to even count her as a friend. Myrna was too private a person to get close to. Maybe it was just as well to go back home. I was about to curl up in a sad heap on my cot, when Adele came in. She gave me a caring look then she sat down and put her arm around my shoulder. I wrapped my arms around her, bawling, letting loose all my disappointment.

All she said was, "There, there, we'll get through this." Her comforting words made me appreciate what a good friend she was, after all.

We were in a state of shock. We had only two weeks remaining in service. The next day, the commanding officer at the base announced that we could take out any aircraft we wanted, since it was probably the last time in our entire lives we would ever be able to fly those mighty, military airplanes.

I found Myrna checking out a Thunderbolt. "Hi Myrna, how are you holding up?"

"I'm very sorry to leave the WASPs," she said, looking longingly toward the Thunderbolt.

"I know how you feel. I'm disappointed that we don't get to stay to celebrate the victory when the war does finally end."

"I heard at the base in New Castle that the WASPs offered to continue to work for a dollar a year until the war was over."

"What was the general's answer?" I asked, surprised.

"The answer was no, that there were plenty of men to do the job now," Myrna said, sadly looking down at the long row of grounded planes. "Do you know what Adele said to me?"

"What?"

"'Cheer up, kid. Nothing good ever lasts. The WASPs were just temporary substitutes for the men.'"

"She would say that, though I think she meant well," I said, trying to defend her.

"Yes, like all us gals, we flew for the love of our

country. I sure am going to miss everyone." Myrna looked directly at me for the first time and gave me a warm hug. I kissed her cheek, and then we both went our separate ways, picking out our favorite airplane to take on one last flight.

On our final day, without any fanfare, the Army Airforces flew each of us to the largest city in our state, as close as possible to our homes; then we were on our own from there. I was lucky to be in California. Myrna was dropped off in Minneapolis, 10 hours from her family's country home.

I was glad the train ride from Palm Springs to San Jose took a while, since it gave me time to think about transitioning from the Army back to being at home. From the station, I walked toward home. I felt worn out with despair as I shuffled down the dusty path toward the farmhouse. My legs felt so heavy I could barely make it to the front door. When I opened it, there was Mother, in her familiar floral apron.

She rushed toward me, opened her arms, and held me close. "Violet, dear! I am relieved to have you back home safe and alive."

I was comforted by her unexpected display of affection, and began to cry quietly in her arms. "Thank you, Mother, I'm happy to be home."

Tommy came in with a grin. "Hi, Sis, welcome back." He must have grown a foot. Howie followed him in, looking older, also.

After I kissed them both, they scurried outside. I watched Mother sweeping the floor and said, "I just don't know what I'm going to do with my life."

"Just take your time, honey," she said with compassion. "We're all glad to have you back. Why don't you go out and say hello to your father? He'd love to see you."

All I did was nod and went sulking into my room. I sat on my bed, turning the pages of my old *Air Today* magazine. Mother had never in my life called me "honey" — only Dad had used that endearment. Maybe being home would work out for me, after all.

Eight months dragged by, and I was getting bored helping Mother around the house. I smelled Dad's cigar and went into the living room. Naturally, the Zenith was tuned in. The radio broadcast sounded like a party.

"What's all the celebration on the news about, Dad?" I asked, sitting on the other side of the radio.

"Shhhush, honey, just listen up," he answered with a long pull on his cigar.

"Ladies and Gentlemen, the war is over! It is victory over Japan! In New York City, all the servicemen are grabbing and kissing every gal in sight, and the girls are willingly kissing

them right back! The bars are packed; everyone is celebrating the winning side just like after one big, giant football game. Now for a speech from President Harry S. Truman..."

"Martha, come listen to this broadcast. Praise be to God, the war is over at last!" Dad said.

My head was spinning. Snippets of the president's speech mingled with my thoughts.

"My Fellow Americans, the Japanese have officially laid down their arms..."

I thought of my friends in the WASPs.

"They have signed terms of unconditional surrender..."

I thought of Lana and Glenn as the president's words blared over the radio.

"We shall never forget Pearl Harbor..."

Our little town held a parade a few days later, though I couldn't bring myself to participate. I wished I had been at the base when the end of the war was announced. I imagined what a wonderful party we could have had in the Officers' Club. I missed the camaraderie of the WASPs.

Mother handed me a letter. I curiously tore it open.

```
Capitol Airlines

Los Angeles, California

Dear Miss Willey:
```

Our company would like to invite former Women Airforce Service Pilots to apply for employment as airline stewardesses. We have several positions available. Please contact the above address if you are interested.

"Who is it from, dear?" Mother asked.

Making a paper airplane out of the letter, I sailed it into the living room, laughing. "And can you use a good upstairs maid with 800 flying hours?" I choked out a fake laugh.

"Honey, why don't you go back to college? It could be a new beginning for you." She patted my shoulder.

I stormed off to my room. Lying on my bed, staring up at the ceiling, I thought maybe I should go back to school. It wouldn't be too hard to live at home now that Mother and I were much closer.

The next morning, I got up early to remove my hair-rollers. I parted my light blond hair on the side, and rolled a curl in a wide circle on top of my head. Taking a hairpin out of my mouth, I tucked in the curl, and secured it in place. I repeated the process with the other side of my head. I swept up the rest in the back, which took about five more hairpins. I turned my head from side to side and admired my new Victory Roll in the mirror. *A new beginning,* I thought, forcing a toothy smile and fluffing up the rolls of my hairdo.

Toward the middle of September, I enrolled full-time in General Education at San Jose State College. Unfortunately, the classes didn't seem to give me any inspiration as to what I wanted to do with the rest of my life. Losing my fiancé and my best friend still weighed heavily on me. A cloud of depression hung about, no matter how hard I tried to shake it. But one day, as I passed by the same bulletin board that had announced the Civil Pilot Training Program a few years before, a flyer caught my eye.

Women's Veterans of War Club

Come join our group every Tuesday at 12:00 noon

Meet in Room 720

Brookhaven Building

I needed a boost. It might be helpful to talk to other women who had experienced as much death as I had. Maybe I could make some new friends with common interests.

Tuesday rolled around and my mood lifted slightly as I entered Room 720. There were over 30 women in the room. I was a little late, but was greeted warmly by everyone.

"Hello, my name is Loretta Mandel, and this is the first meeting of our veterans' support group. Welcome."

"Thank you," I said, shyly averting my eyes as I slipped into the second row.

"Let's start with the front row, ladies. Please state your name, what branch of the military you were in, and your duties."

Most of the women were typists, cooks, and there was one Naval nurse. My turn came and I proudly stated, "My name is Violet Willey, and I worked for the Army Airforces as a ferry pilot."

An uncomfortable silence descended over the room. The leader looked directly into my eyes. "A ferry pilot? There were no women pilots during the war."

"I flew over 35 types of military airplanes from the factories to the bases for our men to fly overseas into combat," I said with pride.

Miss Mandel asked, "You were in the Army Airforces?"

"No, I'm afraid not. The women ferry pilots were paid by Civil Service. The Costello Bill that was presented to Congress to allow the Women Airforce Service Pilots to be part of the Army was marginally defeated last year."

All the women whispered and murmured to each other. Miss Mandel said, "Well, Miss Willey, I'm sorry, but you won't be able to join our club, since you were not in any branch of the service."

My mouth dropped open, my mind racing furiously. I couldn't think of anything to say. I hung my head and slinked out of the room.

Riding home on the bus, I felt like crying, but I couldn't find any tears left in me. Dejected, I walked into the pasture. I thought I heard an old Curtiss Jenny in the sky. Looking across the horizon, I saw a long, cirrus horsetail cloud. No, it was just a commercial airplane. A loud clattering told me that Dad was plowing the fields on his tractor. I looked closely at the back of his head and noticed that there appeared to be more gray than brown. I pushed my curls higher on my head, redoing some of the hairpins. Optimism rushed into my thoughts. What did I want to do with my life? The answer slowly descended upon me. I would love to take flight instructor classes at the town airport and teach Dad to fly! After all, he might not have many years left. I imagined Dad's joy as he soared high above the clouds, me by his side, filled with the same delight we shared the first time in a Jenny.

This sudden inspiration relaxed my face into a dreamy smile as the hot sun of September warmed my soul.

Epilogue

After the War ended, there was a long list of WASPs looking for jobs in the sky.

Violet Willey obtained money to get her flight instructor's license by being a receptionist at the airport. After acquiring it, she taught clients to fly, as a substitute when the male instructors were absent. At age 70, she flew in an around-the-world air race.

Adele Watts went to college and worked part-time in her family's grocery store. It took her 10 years to get her PhD in Aviation Education, since there was no GI Bill available for WASPs to pay for college.

Myrna Gadd ran an airline reservations department after unsuccessfully applying to work as a pilot for the airline companies. Only men were hired. After remarrying a pilot and having a baby, in 1975, her oldest daughter became a commercial airline captain.

Rosemary Wright went to seminary school and became an Episcopal Priest.

Mei-lee Wong became an engineer for an aircraft company, designing helicopter cockpits. She co-authored a book about snakes.

Esther Calhoun worked in an assembly aircraft plant, and later helped start a flying school and an organization for black pilots in Chicago.

Harry Willey got his pilot's license at age 56 from his

daughter, Violet. At age 72, he bought his own four-place Fairchild airplane.

Tommy Willey became manager of the San Jose Airport.

Howie Willey became a successful real estate investor.

Lieutenant Lydia Levacoff shot down a total of 12 enemy planes, and was wounded two different times before she perished. Her family received the highest Soviet military decoration, the "Gold Star Hero of the Soviet Union" medal.

Officer Sonya Bersova was wounded once. After the war, she married, had two sons, and never flew again.

Jacqueline Cochran, (5/11/1906-8/9/1980) director of the Women Airforce Service Pilots, supervised the training of hundreds of women pilots at Avenger Field, Sweetwater Texas. She received the Distinguished Service Medal and the Distinguished Flying Cross.

At the end of the war she was a global reporter, where she witnessed Japanese General Yasmashita's surrender in the Philippines, and was the first non-Japanese woman to enter Japan after the war. Ms. Cochran attended the Nuremberg Trials in Germany. In 1948, Cochran joined the U.S. Air Force Reserve where she rose to the rank of Lieutenant Colonel. Jacqueline Cochran was the first woman to accomplish many feats:

- Flew a bomber across the North Atlantic (1941)

- Broke the sound barrier (1953)

- Landed and took off from an aircraft carrier

- Made a blind instrument landing

- President of the Federation Aeronautique International (1958-1961)

- Flew the Goodyear Blimp with Captain R.W. Crosier in Akron, Ohio

- Flew a fixed-wing jet aircraft across the Atlantic

- Flew above 20,000 feet with an oxygen mask

- Entered the Bendix Transcontinental Race

- A crater on the planet Venus was named after her (1985)

- Honored with a permanent display of her achievements at the United States Air Force Academy (1996)

- The United States Post Office honored her with a postage stamp

- Inducted into the Motorsports Hall of Fame of America (1993)

- There is an open public airport named after Jacqueline Cochran near Palm Springs, California called *Jacqueline Cochran Regional Airport,* as well as an annual air show called the *Jacqueline Cochran Air Show.*

Jacqueline Cochran holds more distance and speed records than any pilot living or dead, male or female.

History of the Women Airforce Service Pilots

Great Britain used women to ferry planes as part of the Air Transport Auxiliary. Eight women began ferrying single-engine Tiger Moth trainers around England in 1940. Many women joined the program from Poland, Chile, and the United States. In March 1942, Jacqueline Cochran took 25 women to England to fly with the British ATA. They flew Spitfires, Typhoons, Hurricanes, Mitchells, and Blenheims from the factories to RAF bases all over England. Even though this was a non-combat role, the chance of being shot down or bombed by the enemy still existed for these pilots.

There were two groups of women ferry pilots. The Women's Flying Training Detachment (WFTD), headed by Jacqueline Cochran and The Women's Auxiliary Ferrying Squadron (WAFS), headed by Nancy Harkness Love. They required only 35 hours of flight training and a minimum age of 18 years old.

Both of these groups joined together to make up the Women Airforce Service Pilots. It was established on August 5, 1943. The WASPs required 1,400 flying hours and a commercial pilot rating with a minimum age of 21.

The director, Jacqueline Cochran, presented a bill to become part of the Army Airforce in order to give military status to the WASPs. The House of Representatives defeated the bill by a narrow margin on

June 21, 1944.

The House Committee on Civil Service presented a report stating that continued recruiting and training of women pilots was wasteful and should be terminated, as returning male pilots should be able to fill all flying assignments.

The Women Airforce Service Pilots program was deactivated on December 20th, 1944, eight months before the war was over. The WASPs were devastated by this news. One group offered to remain in service for $1.00 a year, but their offer was turned down. They did not get to participate in the celebration of the end of the war.

- 25,000 women applied to the WASPs

- 1,830 women entered for WASP training

- 1,074 graduated from the WASPs

- 407 women were injured

- 38 gave their lives in service, 11 in training and 27 on active duty

- There were two documented acts of sabotage by American male mechanics

- The WASPs were assigned to over 134 bases

- They flew 77 types of airplanes with a total of 60,000,000 miles

- The WASPs delivered 12,652 planes of 78 different types

- Two Chinese American women were in the

WASPs; Hazel Ying Lee (died in a runway collision on duty) and Maggie Gee.

- One Native American woman was a ferry pilot, Ola Mildred Rexroat.

- There were no African Americans accepted into the WASPs.

- The WASPs had a statistically proven lower rate of accidents than male cadets.

In 1948, President Harry Truman ended segregation in the Armed Forces.

A broadcast in the 1970s announced that the Air Force planned to train its first women military pilots. This false statement caused a group of retired WASPs to collect signatures, lobbying Congress to pass a bill to grant military status to the WASPs after 33 years. Senator Barry Goldwater, a former World War II ferry pilot in the 27th Ferry Squadron, supported the bill.

On November 23, 1977, President Carter signed legislation #95-202, section 401, The GI Bill Improvement Act of 1977, granting the WASPs full military status for their service.

In 1973, Emily Warner was the first commercial woman airline pilot to fly for Frontier Airlines, Denver, Colorado.

In 1976, the Air Force allowed women pilot training.

In 1984, every WASP was awarded the World War II Victory Medal and American Theater Ribbon/American

Campaign Medal.

President Barack Obama and the United States Congress awarded the WASPs the Congressional Gold Medal. During the ceremony on 3/10/2010, President Obama said, "The Women Airforce Service Pilots courageously answered their country's call in a time of need while blazing a trail for the brave women who have given and continue to give so much in service to this nation since." He further stated: "Every American should be grateful for their service, and I am honored to sign this bill to finally give them some of the hard-earned recognition they deserve."

President Obama signs the bill awarding the Congressional Gold Medal, the highest civilian award presented by the U.S. Congress

Madge Moore showing the WASP Congressional Gold Medal

In 1993, women were allowed to participate in combat flying.

There are approximately 300 surviving WASPs.

History of the Soviet 588ᵗʰ Women's Night Bombers Regiment

The Soviet Union was the first nation to use women pilots.

They flew 23,000 combat missions, 15-18 missions a night.

There were 400 women pilots, 30 of whom died in service.

They flew 1,100 nights of combat.

The Gold Star Hero of the Soviet Union, their nation's highest award, was given to 23 members.

America sent 14,795 aircraft to the Soviet Union during the war.

In 1990, 50 WASPs went to the Soviet Union to meet some of the Night Witches.

About the Author

Photo by Star Dewar

Author Jeane Slone is the daughter of parents who served in the Army during World War II. She has flown in a 1918 World War I Curtiss Jenny (one of only 10 presently airborne).

Ms. Slone has experienced the following aerobatic maneuvers: the Loop, Barrel Roll, Hammer Head, and Cuban Eight in a 1941 World War II Boeing PT-17 Stearman open-cockpit biplane.

Jeane Slone is a member of The Healdsburg Literary Guild, The Redwood Writer's Club, and The Military Writers Society of America.

In 2009, Ms. Slone received a grant from The Sonoma

County Arts Council and gathered six former WASPs for a panel discussion. The Sonoma County Media Center produced a DVD of the standing-room-only event. The DVD is available for purchase on her web site.

Ms. Slone's second historical fiction is titled, *She Built Ships During World War II.* What do the Port Chicago explosion, Tuskegee Airmen, Japanese American internment, women welders, and riveters have in common? This historical fiction weaves all of those events into one fast-paced novel. The reader is immersed into the era of the '40s on the home front, following three diverse women as they experience gender and ethnic discrimination in a man's world.

Ms. Slone's third historical fiction is titled, *She Was An American Spy During World War II.* This book tells the reader how young women were recruited to become spies, what "spy camp" was like, and the missions women were sent on.

Visit: www.JeaneSlone.com

Email: info@jeaneslone.com